Music Lessons

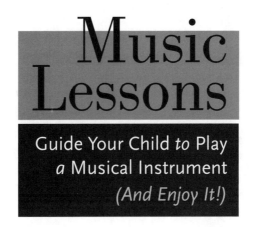

Music Lessons

Guide Your Child *to* Play *a* Musical Instrument
(And Enjoy It!)

Stephanie Stein Crease

CHICAGO
REVIEW
PRESS

784.193
Ste

Library of Congress Cataloging-in-Publication Data

Stein Crease, Stephanie.
  Music lessons : guide your child to play a musical instrument (and
enjoy it!) / by Stephanie Stein Crease.— 1st ed.
    p. cm.
  Includes bibliographical references (p.   ) and index.
  ISBN-13: 978-1-55652-604-6
  ISBN-10: 1-55652-604-0
 1. Musical instrument selection for children. 2. Music—Instruction
and study. I. Title.
  MT740.S74 2006
  784.193085—dc22

                                                                    2006006752

Cover and interior design: Sarah Olson
Cover photo: David Sacks, Image Bank/Getty Images

Photo credits: on pp. 1 and 62, photos by Robert P. Crease; on p. 44,
photo by Dan Townley; on pp. 71, 92, 132, and 152, photos by Ellen
Brofman, courtesy of InterSchool Orchestras of New York; on pp. 107
and 114, photos by Yoshie Yoshimune; on pp. 149 and 159, photos courtesy of InterSchool Orchestras of New York. All rights reserved.

© 2006 by Stephanie Stein Crease
All rights reserved
First edition
Published by Chicago Review Press, Incorporated
814 North Franklin Street
Chicago, Illinois 60610
ISBN-13: 978-1-55652-604-6
ISBN-10: 1-55652-604-0
Printed in the United States of America
5 4 3 2 1

Contents

꩜

To R.P.C.
—ever attuned to the sounds of surprise

Acknowledgments

Just as it may take a village to raise a child, writing a book such as this also takes a village.

I would like to extend my deepest gratitude to senior editor Yuval Taylor, who remained patient, enthusiastic, and insightful through the entire process of completing this book. Also, very special thanks to my agent Susan Ramer, who confidently and patiently helped me follow through with this project. My sincere thanks also goes to Lisa Rosenthal, editor, and Gerilee Hundt, managing editor, Allison Felus, and the entire editorial, design, and production staff at Chicago Review Press, who carefully guided this book into print.

I would like to especially acknowledge those who read the manuscript in its entirety or portions thereof: Kathy Allen, Robert Crease, Emily King, Karen Oberlin, and Eve Weiss.

There are many other people—children and adults—who helped contribute to this book in ways large and small. Very special thanks to the entire staff of the InterSchool Orchestras of New York, especially Annabelle Prager, founder; Ann McKinney, director; Ellen Brofman, education director; Robert Johnson, conductor; and all the children and families of the Morningside and Carnegie Hill Orchestras.

My profound gratitude also goes to the following individuals, families, and organizations: Sam Amidon; Peter Amidon; Johnella and Khalil Blassingame; Erich Bachrach, director, Community Music School of Springfield (Massachusetts); Andrew Brito and Marisol Cuevas; David Carleton and Shelley Greenberg, Turtle Bay Music School; Naomi Cohen; Brenda Dillon; Anne Farber and Cynthia Lilley, Dalcroze School at Lucy Moses; Barry Goldberg, executive director of the New York Youth Symphony; Chris Jenkins; Larry Malin; Ariel and Shelley Mitnick; Paula Robison; Linda Rainwater; Ann Roberts; Lydia Ross; Tamara Litt and the Litt Family; Felice Swados; Jonathan Russell and his family; Jo Shifter, North Shore Suzuki, Stony Brook, New York; and Mizuho and Yoshie Yoshimune.

Lastly, I would like to thank my son Alexander Crease, whose joyful noise and music making inspired this book, my extension child India Schneider-Crease, and my husband Robert P. Crease—philosopher, writer, and historian. This project would not have come to pass without his care and support, his insight, goodwill, and great sense of humor—through thick and thin.

Introduction

Last spring, I attended the annual talent show at my son's elementary school in New York City. The majority of the fifty or so acts consisted of children lip-synching to their favorite songs. Or, more likely, to their parents' favorite songs. There were a lot of Beatles songs, for instance—and the opening act was a kindergartner who mouthed the words to the Doors' "Break on Through."

But it was a tiny second grader who brought down the house. Sitting at the auditorium's battered piano, she adeptly swept through a Chopin nocturne. Her schoolmates, aware that she was doing something magnificent, rushed downstage and crowded around her, screaming with even more glee and pride than at their lip-synching friends.

Anna Chen was one of only seven children who performed classical music that night. All seven are engaged in music strictly on an extracurricular basis. Though my son's school is one of the top-ranked public schools in New York City, it offers no instrumental instruction and has no chorus. Its part-time music teacher, whose salary is paid for by the PTA, lost her classroom last year. In addition to those obstacles, her curriculum, to those of us with any musical background, is disheartening: her instruction in music notation rarely progresses beyond an introduction, and the children learn folk songs from around the world but never hear a snippet of Mozart or Beethoven, let alone Aaron Copland or Duke Ellington.

Unfortunately, this kind of hazy curriculum passes for music education in many public schools today. Why is this so? There are several reasons. In the 1970s, budget cuts took a devastating toll on general music instruction and instrumental music programs across the country. In the decades since, reinstating any kind of music education in public schools has been erratic and dependent on local economics, attitudes, politics, school boards, and the interest and commitment of individual school principals. The 2001 federal No Child Left Behind Act, which mandates improving basic literacy and math skills (though the act's long-term success has yet to be borne out), has once again relegated music and other subjects to the back burner in many schools. Sadly, there is not a No Child Left Behind policy for music education, though numerous studies point to the academic benefits of learning a musical instrument.

Some states, particularly in the northeast, have made gains to re-create music programs, often with the help of outreach organizations, partnerships with cultural institutions, and parent-led initiatives. In other states, music instruction is still in decline. Yet data from a national 1999–2000 survey of approximately 1,200 public schools (six hundred elementary schools and six hundred secondary) look promising. Conducted by the National Center for Education Statistics (NCES), this was the first national survey to address arts education in our public schools. The results (compiled from a questionnaire answered by school principals and music teachers) indicate that over 93 percent of elementary school students receive some form of music instruction, and 90 percent of secondary school students have the opportunity to take a music elective. But a spokesperson for the National Alliance for Music Education said that, more likely, 45 percent to 50 percent of elementary school students are not getting adequate music instruction—or anything closely resembling the comprehensive K–12 music curriculum as outlined in the National Standards for Music Education.

It's even more difficult to capture accurate statistics for the number of children involved in hands-on instrumental instruction, such as band, orchestra, or string programs. General music classes in elementary school are geared for all students, but string, orchestra, and band programs were only offered in about one third of the schools surveyed, and even then they're typically offered only to students in grade four and up, as an elective, and on a limited basis. Big-city schools can rarely accommodate all students and often struggle to provide decent instruments. The result? A void in music instruction, which nurtures other aspects of learning such as physical coordination, cognitive development, and cultural literacy.

Music Lessons will help you fill this void. It explains how parents, who may have little musical background themselves, can initiate and nurture their children's musical education with the labor-of-love process of learning musical instruments. It will help you acculturate yourselves and your children to the rich legacy of classical and twentieth-century music that may not ordinarily be part of your family's sound world. It will guide your family to make informed choices— of instruments, programs, and instructors—that will provide the best fit for your children. It will also help you become better informed about what kind of music instruction your child is or is not receiving in school and provide information about organizations dedicated to improving music education in our schools.

The first few chapters address parents' foremost concerns about music and instrumental instruction. In our pop, rap, and hip-hop–saturated musical world, why bother to study classical music or even to learn to read musical notation? Can all children benefit from this kind of instruction? Does it matter if your child is musical—and how do you know? How do you choose an instrument or a teacher? What is the right age to start a particular instrument? What are the expenses for music lessons? Can you afford them? When do you take a child to hear a first symphonic concert or a first jazz concert?

Music Lessons can also help parents avoid the negative experiences many of us had with piano teachers who were too strict or spent a lot of time on uninspiring repertoire. It offers key guidance to one of the trickiest hurdles of all: helping our children learn how to practice daily (or almost daily). It will also help parents with another common hurdle—when your child emphatically says that he or she wants to quit. Every chapter ends with a list of resources that includes recommended reading and listening, as well as organizations and Web sites for further exploration of the covered topics.

Admittedly, some of this information may sound like nothing more than good parenting common sense. But whether we are musically trained parents or not, our sound reasoning and good intentions can easily go off track. For instance, the piano is considered an excellent first instrument for children for its ease of obtaining pleasing sounds and its visible logic of note placement. For many children, though, the novelty of private piano lessons wears off quickly, eroded by the child's feeling that practice is a solitary activity and often a struggle; soon, he or she is begging to quit. A possible solution? Switch gears, at least for a while, but don't give up. Learning to play music with other children may be a better choice for your child and a more immediately motivating one. Learning to play the recorder in a group may be a better choice for the moment, since it often provides both a positive experience and a chance to acquire transferable skills that may lead to the mastery of a more challenging instrument later on.

My aim is to help parents find the right balance of support, continuity, and flexibility to follow through with this process. The result? Children will indeed relish their own musical progress. They will become comfortable with the physicality of their instruments and will master repertoire that at first seemed daunting. Practice does reach a magic vortex, when the child's concept of his or her own musicality and skills becomes self-gratifying and self-motivating.

Demystifying Classical Music and Instruments

My parents' eclectic listening habits gave me a lifelong love of and curiosity about all kinds of music. The radio or stereo was almost always on when I walked into the house: the music of Beethoven, Leonard Bernstein, Billie Holiday, or the Beatles is forever entwined with my sense of home. I have passed this eclectic mind-set on to my ten-year-old son, who is as fascinated as I was by the signature styles of different performers and composers and by orchestral music—its power, grandeur, drama, and the complexity of beautiful sounds.

My son's developing musicality inspired me to delve more deeply into the subject of children's musical upbringing. His formal musical education started far earlier than I anticipated it would, and it started on the violin, an instrument I still find mystifying and difficult. When he was three and a half years old, I took him to a children's violin concert, and for days afterward, "Mommy, I want to play the violin!" was a new refrain in our house. He soon joined the ranks of preschool Suzuki violin students. Until then, I had imagined him studying piano as his first instrument—and as a much older child.

What compelled me to follow his interest? I trusted his fascination with the instrument and his early conception of himself making music. Though not without struggles, my son's musicianship is flourishing. He walks around singing or whistling his current repertoire, will eagerly practice what he's keen to learn, and proudly performs his favorite pieces for his friends: themes from the Harry Potter movies, old-time American fiddle tunes (played at breakneck speed), and a whimsical gavotte with a tricky trill.

The fact that his repertoire has become more eclectic is no accident. His joy in mastering a fast fiddle tune spills over to wanting to perfect that tricky trill, and both his teacher and I encourage this beneficial crossover. Duke Ellington often said that good music is "beyond category." Engaging your child's interest in different styles of music—be it jazz, country, or pop—while encouraging the sound musicianship and good technique that goes hand in hand with learning to play instruments using classical repertoire and methods are cornerstones of this book.

Two key aspects of the musical learning process often get minimal emphasis, even from music teachers. The first is that classical music, twentieth-century music, and jazz are marginalized in America. Our children hear pop, rap, rock, and various blends of world music when they're just walking around—on television, on radio, in stores, at malls, and in the movies. But radio stations that used to feature classical music have suffered cutbacks in many locales, and exposure to classical music and orchestral instruments in school is no longer a given. So if your child will be playing pieces by Mozart and Bach, or by the Beatles and Duke Ellington, try to include this music as part of your family's everyday listening experience. Familiarize yourself with music you and your children can enjoy together: dance to *Bolero* and *West Side Story*, hum along to *Peter and the Wolf*, and sing to Beethoven's Sixth (remember *Fantasia?*). This will help your child develop a keen enjoyment and knowledge of all kinds of music.

The second key aspect is that learning an instrument takes tremendous dedication. Especially for young children starting out, a parent or caregiver will need to be the child's primary musical partner. At home, the adult partner can reinforce what was learned in the lesson and, with the help of the teacher, establish practice routines that are age-appropriate, skill-enhancing, and fun. As parents, we need to accentuate the positive, for things small and large ("Good bow hold!" or "Wow, you played the whole piece!"). For ourselves, we need to develop large reserves of patience and good humor.

The Early Ear

This book is primarily targeted for children between the ages of three and ten, but it also includes useful information for toddlers, and for teenagers who are suddenly inspired to learn an instrument.

A number of classically oriented methods and programs commonly taught to young children (including preschoolers) are discussed here. The Suzuki Method is based on an engaging imitative ear-training approach, with very young children using small-scale violins and cellos. At some Suzuki programs, the method is taught for piano and even flute. Playing and learning together, in addition to private lessons, are significant components of the Suzuki method, so early in the process, children are placed in ensembles. The Orff Schulwerk approach, created by the German composer Carl Orff and his colleagues, also utilizes playing and learning in ensembles, with specially devised xylophones, other percussion instruments, and recorders. Dalcroze training encourages a "whole body" approach to developing musical skills, through expressive movement, voice and ear training, and improvisation. Though Orff Schulwerk and Dalcroze are not instrumental methods per se, both approaches help the child develop skills that lead easily to traditional instrumental instruction later on.

Mainly, this book is an invitation to parents and musically minded children. Nurturing the high-expectation experience inherent in learning a musical instrument is a gift to your child. It spills into several areas crucial to child development: small motor skills, mathematical thinking, memory retention, self-discipline, enhanced spatial and temporal awareness, and concentration, among others. The effort—for parent and child—pays off. My son's experiences with incremental learning and performing with other children yielded rich rewards early on: mastering material that at first seemed difficult; experiencing performance as a natural, joyful activity; and discovering cultural and historical connections ("Beethoven's favorite food was macaroni and cheese!").

But the benefits of music in one's daily life need no spill-over justifications. The communicative and creative aspects of making music are age-old and reach deep into every culture and our humanity. Playing musical instruments provides children with a channel for emotional expression, for reenacting rituals and celebrations, and for creating something beautiful with other people through cooperation and guided mindfulness.

This book is not a professional manual. It is not for parents who want their children to become professional musicians. It is for those parents who believe that a musical experience is vital to a well-formed child, no matter what kind of music that child grows into liking. My son's schoolmate Anna Chen may well front a hip-hop band some day—but the impassioned discipline, skill, and joy she displayed at the battered auditorium piano will provide great training for her future and will resonate throughout her life.

Music
Lessons

The Early Ear, Ages Two to Five

It's a Saturday morning in October. Sunlight streams in the windows of a large room in a church basement, lending warmth to an already brisk fall day. Parents are seated on folding chairs, some reading, some attentive, some napping, some struggling to keep their babies quiet. In the center of the room, a dynamic woman in her early sixties stands in front of twelve children, all between three and four years old, arrayed in a half-circle facing  her. She is holding a violin bow, using sweeping gestures to accompany the words of a rhyme, demonstrating how to keep a steady handgrip on the bow while the arm is moving. The children hold tiny bows—some as small as eight inches—and chant along with her, mimicking her actions.

Up like a rocket, down like the rain
    [moves bow straight up and down]
back and forth like a choo-choo train
    [moves bow horizontally]
'round and 'round we go like the sun
    [makes a large circular movement]
up on our heads and now we're done.
    [moves straight up to top of head]

This is a Suzuki violin class, one of the first that this group of children have had together. While copying the teacher's movements, the children engage their bodies in the chant's rhythm. Like other Suzuki rhymes, chants, and games for beginners, it is a purposeful exercise to help students develop coordination for the small and large movements needed for playing their violins and to help them move with a steady rhythm. The teacher points out who is holding the bow correctly and gently adjusts the children whose hand positions are not quite right.

The thirty-minute lesson is playful. Children march around the room with their bows, learn to move rhythmically in unison, sing the unofficial Suzuki anthem, "Twinkle, Twinkle Little Star," and respectfully bow to their teacher at the end of the class. This ensemble class exemplifies, at a glance, the benefits of the Suzuki Method: the children enjoy doing something novel in a group; the teacher is playful and engaging; and parents are present in the background to support their young children and to absorb the lessons that will need to be repeated at home.

Various paths brought these three- and four-year-olds and their parents to this basement on this beautiful fall morning. Lucas's father, a doctor, who paid much of his way through medical school playing jazz piano, kept noticing how fascinated his son was with musical instruments. Lily's parents wanted to give her all the lessons they never had. Daniel's stay-at-home mom wanted her children to engage in a creative activity that also helps develop self-discipline. All these parents believe that learning to play an instrument will be beneficial to their children, now and for years to come.

This kind of class, familiar to the scores of children who start Suzuki lessons every year, may appear to be these children's first step in music. But children begin their musical introduction in infancy—whether their parents are deliberate about their musical exposure or not.

This chapter addresses how we, as parents, shape our children's musical world, even when they are just babies and toddlers, and how creating a home environment filled with music can kindle a child's musical interest. Included here are descriptions of accessible and popular programs geared to babies, toddlers, and preschoolers.

First Steps

In their earliest years, children are an embodiment of their musical experiences. Fascination with sound, singing, humming, chanting, and moving rhythmically are their natural activities and responses to the world. Newborns turn toward a human voice, seeking the source of the sound; within days they can distinguish their mother's voice from that of others. Musical explorations and interactions with sound help babies and toddlers develop linguistic and other cognitive skills. Indeed, very young children are capable of developing critical thinking, some of which stems from learning to interpret "motherese"—a term psychologists coined for the very musical, expressive way that parents, particularly mothers, and other caregivers speak to children. Babies' mimicry of sound and rhythm are the building blocks for language acquisition—and also for the musically educated child.

Psychologists are finding that hearing song is one of the fundamental ways that babies learn to recognize the tones that add up to spoken language. By channeling and creating opportunities for musical processes—active listening, responding to music, and creating sounds and rhythms—parents can help their children build a lifelong involvement with music.

During infancy and early childhood, parents are the main gatekeepers of their children's listening and musical experiences. Parents with musical training or inclinations often replicate their own positive experiences: they sing frequently, point out pleasing sounds in nature, and play a variety of music in the house or car while naming instruments as they hear them. Spontaneous interactive listening and music making of any kind can be, for some households, as natural and essential to their family life as having a pet.

For other parents, their young child's relentless fascination with music and sound inspires them to follow through on behalf of their child, and may kindle their own interest in music. For still others, the current widespread belief that children benefit from studying a musical instrument may encourage them to steer their children toward formal music activities or lessons. A 2002–2003 Gallup Poll conducted to gauge attitudes toward music participation found that a large majority of the 1,000 households surveyed believe that music is an important part of life, that it brings families together, and that playing an instrument is fun and relaxing and can provide a sense of accomplishment. Eighty percent of respondents "completely or mostly agree that making music makes you smarter." (This was the first time this question was included in this poll.)

Many conversations with parents about studying music today inevitably turn to higher SAT scores or how studying music can even enlarge one's brain. But whatever prompted your decision to include music prominently in your child's life, creating a musical environment in your home is the best way to begin. Singing, making and playing simple musical instruments, active listening, and moving to music are exploratory and experiential ways for children to acquire a musical sensibility that can easily be transformed into musical skill in the future.

The following suggestions are easy ways for you to incorporate more music into your home and your young child's world.

♪ Listen with new ears: if you've been a rock 'n' roll fan for most of your adult life, try making orchestral music an everyday listening experience for your family.

♪ Familiarize yourself with music you and your children can enjoy together: dance to Ravel's *Bolero* and Bernstein's *West Side Story*; hum along to Prokofiev's *Peter and the Wolf*; act out the fight in Beethoven's Fifth; cakewalk to Joplin's "The Entertainer."

♪ Follow the suggestions of *Sesame Street*'s Bob McGrath: try to listen to a few minutes of a different piece of music every day with your child and then play these pieces for your child repeatedly over the next few weeks until the music sinks in.

♪ Keep the beat: encourage your kids to bang on a can, move their limbs, and dance! Make a treasure chest of percussion instruments such as homemade rattles and shakers, wood blocks, and cymbals. Invite friends over for a rhythm parade.

♪ Sing, sing, sing! Don't worry about singing in tune or what kind of voice you have. Make singing part of your child's daily routine. You can do this while you're moving from one place or activity to another, between lunchtime and nap time, or while you're riding in the car.

Early childhood is an ideal time to expose children to all kinds of music. It can be classical, jazz, folk—any variety of repertoire and instrumentation that is melodic and appealing. (Fortunately, musical categories such as "smooth jazz," "hard rock," "soft rock," and so forth, which are imposed on us by radio stations and other media, have *no* meaning for young children.) Two- and three-year-olds will recognize music that is played for them frequently; they will sing along with it, hum it, dance to it, ask to hear certain songs again and again, and make the music completely their own.

Responsive Listening

Key listening experiences can be profound for young children and have a lasting influence that is as vivid as other powerful pivotal memories, such as swimming in the ocean for the first time or learning to ride a bike. I still have crystal clear memories of listening to a recording of *Peter and the Wolf* as a four-year-old, with my mother pointing out the instruments/animals as they magically appeared, as if I could see with my ears.

In fact, the moments when children respond deeply to music can have a positive impact on their future musical development. In one of his studies, Dr. John Sloboda, a British psychologist who has conducted extensive research with high-achieving musicians, found that young children can have intense emotional responses to music, which later provide them with a strong motivation to both learn an instrument and play it with great expression. These experiences tend to occur in relaxed environments where "nothing is being asked of the child," when the child may be listening to music at home with his family or friends—not while performing or in the presence of a teacher.

Musicality in children also develops from active, participatory listening situations. What makes listening active? Singing along, tapping, clapping, pounding out rhythms, pointing out the sounds and names of instruments, and explaining how the music might tell a story, even without words. Playing conductor to recordings, dancing, and moving rhythmically to music are all ways to be active participants in music with your children.

These activities can expand as your child becomes increasingly more aware of what he or she is hearing. Ask your child questions about the music. Does it sound happy or sad? Is the sound high or low? Loud or soft? Can you sing along with it? Can you sing that note, play that rhythm? Very young children delight in repetition; repeating choruses or singing the same song a zillion times is all part of the process. At this stage, there is no reason to be concerned if a child (or you) sings out of tune. Your child will get great pleasure from mirroring the music, as he or she does with so much else in life. More accurate replications of pitch and rhythm will follow, with repetition and as the child matures. These kinds of listening activities make music central to your children's everyday experience and can help inspire them to keep up their interest later on, when they are ready to start instrumental instruction.

Attend Live Musical Events

Most communities offer musical performances or events that are child friendly. That means a certain amount of noise is expected, and people can come and go without worrying about disturbing others. From the time our son was just a few months old, we took him to fiddle festivals, concerts featuring other children, and family programs at the New York Philharmonic, where noise from offstage didn't raise any eyebrows. A child's exposure to the sound and sight of real people playing real instruments together can be a joyful and dynamic experience. Casual concert settings also prepare your child to attend more grown-up concerts in the future, where sitting quietly is expected. Children quickly learn that they are taking part in something special, something that's worth sitting still (or *mostly* still) for.

Many community musical events are free or inexpensive and well worth seeking out. For example, check out musical offerings at your local library, community music school, and university; look out especially for concerts featuring young performers, such as Suzuki concerts or holiday concerts by a local youth orchestra.

Almost every American symphony orchestra currently presents affordable family concerts to attract young, new, and future audiences. The Seattle Symphony has a Tiny Tots series of three hour-long thematic concerts for children under five (babies welcome!), in addition to a more typical symphonic series designed for five- to twelve-year-olds. Another example is the historic Young People at the Philharmonic series in New York City, with ticket prices that range from $8 to $25. Many family concerts host an array of hands-on preconcert activities, with opportunities to try out different instruments, make simple instruments, make reeds out of straws, and so forth, which get the children excited about the concert itself.

Next Steps

How do you recognize whether your child is ready for something beyond the home? What programs are available for the preschool set? How can you determine what's right for your child? Should your child start on an instrument? Does it make sense for preschoolers to take private lessons, or is there a group class that might be better suited for eager yet fidgety young children?

Some children are so persistent in their interest in music or a specific instrument that you can't ignore it. This is worth heeding and following up in some way, even if it's a sing-along hour at the library.

Ariel, now a very accomplished thirteen-year-old violinist, first heard a violin up close when she was three. One day Ariel's preschool class was waiting for parents to pick them up early because of a snowstorm, and the teacher asked her teenage daughter to play her violin to entertain the children. Afterward, Ariel said, "Daddy, I need to do that." For weeks, she repeated her interest to both her parents, neither of whom had ever studied an instrument. Her mother resisted doing anything about it because Ariel "was so busy doing all these other little kid activities—ballet, gymnastics. I told her she had to wait a year. About a year later to the day, Ariel came up to me and said, 'It's been a year. I want to do this.'"

Eve, a classical guitar teacher, says that, for some children, the instrument itself is the vehicle. "Some children will see someone play the violin when they're three and that's it! They only want to play the violin—the instrument becomes their passion. With other kids, it might not matter what the instrument is but their interest in music is still really strong. It could be *any* instrument and they will take off on it."

The growing demand for music programs for the very young has risen dramatically over the last two decades, as general attitudes about early childhood development point to the benefits of focusing on music. If your child is fascinated by music, or a particular instrument, then it is probably time to see what's available in your community. Talk to preschool teachers and to other parents to discover what is near your home; see if your area has any community music schools that offer music activity classes for toddlers and preschoolers. In some small-town settings, sing-along hours or other informal music activities are held in public libraries. Observe some classes, both with and without your child, to see how the children are grouped in terms of age and development and what activities take place.

Noteworthy programs, such as Dalcroze, Kindermusik, and Music Together (discussed at length on pages 11 and 12 and in chapter 2 on pages 34–37), have music teachers who have specific early childhood training, in addition to certified training for particular methods. It is wise to consult with directors and teachers of such programs about your child's general readiness and details about the classes (how long they are, and so forth). For three- to five-year-olds, the main idea is to expose your child to engaging musical activities that encourage exploration and are fun for the child.

Bear in mind that all programs for toddlers and preschoolers require the presence and enthusiastic participation of a parent or caregiver. Make sure that you or your child's caregiver is ready to sing, skip around the room, and play simple rhythm instruments.

Here are some early indications of a strong musical interest in your child. Your child:

♪ sings almost constantly, sings along with everything, and often repeats music she has heard

♪ repeats rhythms with a degree of accuracy

♪ persistently plays with any instrument in the house; is able to pick out tunes or melodies

♪ keeps asking to hear familiar pieces of music

Two of the most well-established programs for toddlers and preschoolers—and even babies—are Kindermusik and Music Together. Both programs have become so popular over the last decade that programs and practitioners can be found across the country, anywhere from Kingston, New York, to Eugene, Oregon. The aim of each program is to develop musical awareness and sensitivity through joyful music and movement activities that encourage singing, listening, and a rhythmic sense, and are reinforced with parents at home. Kindermusik was developed in West Germany in the 1960s; it sprang from the Western European classical music tradition and was adapted for use in the United States and other countries. Music Together, which has more of a folk music orientation, was developed by Kenneth Guilmartin, a Dalcroze teacher who founded the Center for Music and Young Children in Princeton, New Jersey, during the mid-1980s. Part of his aim was to design a program to accommodate working parents and their children's caregivers.

Both programs are rooted in the belief that every child is musical. Each program uses carefully sequenced teaching material and offers plenty of backup tapes and CDs for parents and caregivers to nurture a musical environment at home. The materials encourage pitch and rhythmic awareness and a musical sense, all of which help prepare children for music studies later on. Both programs offer an informal atmosphere for toddlers and even infants to engage in relaxed yet exploratory musical playtime.

For one musically trained mother—a first-time parent in her late thirties—the Kindermusik class she and her baby attended offered a different window on child development than did the other Mommy and Me–type classes she tried. "I felt that we were all after something different—that we knew we were giving some tool to these little babies by singing to them together, this big, beautiful, but quiet singing. It was a very gratifying way to be with a group of parents—living in a small town and maybe going a little stir crazy at home."

The Dalcroze and Orff Schulwerk approaches originated in Europe in the first two decades of the twentieth century and are more philosophically and experientially based. Their founders, Émile Jacques Dalcroze and Carl Orff, experimented extensively with how children best learn musical skills and sensitivity (both are discussed in greater detail in chapter 2). Through singing, movement, and using rhythms and percussion instruments, both offer well-founded introductions to music and movement for very young children in ways that purposefully coincide with other aspects of early child development—motor coordination, focusing, and language acquisition. They aim to develop musically aware students with keen listening skills, pitch and rhythmic differentiation, and improvisational ability. Both approaches lay the groundwork for formal instrumental training. In contrast to the above programs, the Suzuki Method is an instrumental method (also discussed in detail in the next chapter). Originally developed as a violin method for children as young as three, Suzuki training has broadened its scope over the years to include cello, piano, trumpet, flute, and, most recently, guitar.

Another trend in recent years is keyboard classes for the very young. One popular, long-established sequential program for four- to nine-year-olds was developed by the Yamaha Music Education System (under the umbrella of Yamaha Corporation, which manufactures acoustic pianos as well as state-of-the-art keyboards and synthesizers). The Armstrong Community Music School in Austin, Texas, formulated its own keyboard program for three- to five-year-olds called Music for Little Mozarts. The advantage of such classes is that, like Suzuki, they rely on learning by ear and imitation; the children play pleasing, easy-to-learn repertoire right away while getting some wonderful early musical exposure. The group setting is appropriate to the age level, and children get the fun, stimulating experience of making music together.

But don't rush your child into a Suzuki program or piano lessons just because she sings all day. Young children may benefit more from ample musical exploration than from our lofty expectations. You might want to consult with program directors or teachers about your child's readiness—particularly if you haven't had experience with formal lessons yourself. And how do you define readiness? Musical eagerness and enjoyment, a good sense of rhythm, good large and small motor coordination, ease in a group setting, and a certain degree of socialization. Can your preschooler listen to the teacher, follow directions, focus for a little while—and enjoy and be engaged by this new experience?

Bear in mind that not every preschool child is ready for classes or lessons, and consider carefully how much you are willing to spend on music education at this time. It's one thing to stretch your budget for an eight-year-old child who shows strong signs of commitment and potential, and another to do so for a musically curious three-year-old. Depending on what area of the country you live in, the fees for early childhood music classes at a community music school can run from two hundred to five hundred dollars for a seventeen-week semester of forty-five-minute classes. Specialized programs like the Suzuki Method can cost between five hundred and seven hundred dollars a semester. However, many programs do have scholarships available, even for very young students. Be sure to research all the options in your community—you may be able to find excellent free or low-cost early childhood music classes. (See chapter 6 for more resources about finding teachers and programs.)

You also need to be honest about your own readiness. Parental involvement is essential for a young child to acquire the skills, routines, and sustained interest that go along with learning to play an instrument. It takes a lot of support and a playful attitude to keep music lessons and practice sessions exploratory and fun. In fact, most Suzuki programs require a parent to learn the violin along with the child for the first year or two, to reinforce what goes on in the lessons, to be a role model, and to instill a sense of joyful expectation about making music. Young Suzuki students learn not just how to play, but also how to practice, even if it's only for ten minutes a day. It's also important for new students to hear music performed beautifully and to experience a variety of music in different settings. It can be particularly inspiring for children to watch older students perform.

A Note About Music Teachers

If you and your child are ready to take the next step, finding the right program and the right teacher are essential. In fact, finding a really special teacher may supersede any other reasons for choosing a specific program. For instance, our son's first Suzuki teacher could miraculously get a group of four-year-olds to listen to her, stay on task, play their little violins together, and still have a good time. She was such a marvel with her young charges, I would have signed up my son to learn *anything* with her.

A child's relationship with her first music teacher can be pivotal for her interest in music. The teacher provides a role model for musicianship and musical involvement and establishes a system for achieving short-term progress that builds toward long-term musicianship. At the same time, a teacher who works with preschoolers and with children in early school grades needs to convey a playful sense of the musical experience—many aspects of learning about music or an instrument can be presented as a puzzle or a game or as something magical. (See chapter 6 for a more detailed discussion on finding the right teacher.)

If and when your child has started private lessons or an instrumental program, pay close attention to his or her reactions and responses during and after a lesson or class. Is the teacher engaging your child's interest? Is the class too long for your child's attention span? Are the expectations of the teacher and the program a good fit at this time? Be sensitive to your child's motor skills, physical comfort, attention span, and—most of all—engagement with the experience.

Ready, Set, Practice!

For the four- or five-year-old who starts an age-appropriate instrument such as violin, piano, or guitar, you will need to establish a practice routine, even if it's only five or ten minutes a day. This is one of the trickiest aspects of instrumental instruction, for parent and child alike. (See chapter 7 for more information about practicing issues.) At this tender stage, practicing should not become a power play, a test of wills, or a torturous experience! Mostly, practicing means working on a few small things every day that will help your child begin to make music and become physically comfortable with his or her instrument. Establishing a routine early on—same time, same place, every day—will help bring your child's musical activity right into the family circle, just like walking the dog or preparing meals together.

Take advantage of your young child's eagerness—children love to please their teachers and their parents by showing off what they are learning. The goal is to reinforce what goes on in the lesson and, ultimately, to enable your child to develop physical control, coordination, and a musical sensibility. This may mean holding the bow correctly, sitting with a good posture at the piano, playing a certain rhythm, all leading up to playing an entire piece such as "Twinkle, Twinkle." Practicing pays off in extramusical ways, too. It helps children learn to break tasks down into small goals, to focus on one thing at a time, to be patient, and to listen to him- or herself.

Practice time, above all, should be a pleasurable time to spend with your child, free of distractions and interruptions. Try to arrange your practice time for when you are both alert and relaxed (not overtired or hungry). The concentrated one-on-one time shared with a parent is a reward in itself for young children.

Here are some ways to get your child to look forward to practice sessions.

♪ Help your child set up a colorful chart for the week.

♪ Use stickers or stars to reward small accomplishments every day.

♪ Make an audience out of stuffed animals or other toys.

♪ Record the practice session. Children delight in hearing themselves, and they can then also hear areas they need to improve.

♪ Have the child pretend to be the teacher and teach you a skill or song.

♪ Make corrections in a supportive, positive way.

♪ Share a favorite snack afterward.

Above all, practicing should be fun at this stage. Use frequent praise for small jobs well done, such as maintaining the right posture or correctly playing through a passage or a whole song. Practicing helps your child learn to concentrate by slowing down enough to focus on the small gestures that add up to making music. What your child is learning goes far beyond the instrument: your child is learning how to learn.

Gifted, Talented, or Tone Deaf?

There is a growing body of evidence suggesting that early musical experience and exposure have a significant effect on later musical ability—even though it might not be observable for years, when a child seems to suddenly make rapid progress on an instrument. Psychologist John Sloboda has long questioned the idea that musicians are born, not made. For Sloboda, the opposite is true: musicians are made, not born. One of his studies indicates that very accomplished conservatory students received far more musical stimulation as babies and children—such as being sung to every day, frequently engaging in song and movement games, and more—than students who did not attain such high levels of technical mastery and expressive ability. In challenging the so-called myth of talent, Sloboda's work stresses the idea that musical ability and achievement can be developed and that nurturing can prevail over nature when ample opportunity, exposure, and encouragement is provided.

Brenda Dillon, a longtime music educator and program director for the National Piano Foundation, agrees with this position.

> I think we need to get away from using the word *talent* in conjunction with music making—it's unfortunate that that was thrown in there. I believe that some of us have an affinity for music, for instance, and we might not have it for math. However, even people who have an affinity still have to go through all the slow repetitions and hard work to learn how to play an instrument. It is painful to hear someone say,

"Well, I would never play music because I just don't have talent." The truth is, we can do anything that we are willing to do slowly, over and over—I find that in all learning. Personally, I believe that we are all programmed to make music. A teacher can nurture that or kill it.

Of course, there is something to be said for recognizing musical affinity and potential. If a child has an unusually strong musical interest, it often will leap out, even at the age of three or four. One such child, named Josef, was already impassioned with the violin at the age of three and a half. His mother was advised to start him with Suzuki training; the traditional violin teachers recommended to her would not take on students so young, or children who could not read yet. Meanwhile, all Josef wanted to do was play violin—he would hear a piece and immediately grapple with figuring out how to play it. His posture, his bowing arm, and his sound all implied a command of the instrument well beyond his years. Neither of his parents played an instrument, but his grandmother was an accomplished pianist, and being musical was a deeply cherished value in the family.

But, like the young violinist Ariel mentioned previously, children with strong potential and an affinity for music can come from families with no musical interest or background. There are several qualities—both musical and personal—that are hard to ignore in a child with an unusually strong musical affinity. He or she would display an excellent sense of pitch and rhythm as well as keen musical retention, and the ability to pick out melodies on a keyboard or other instrument. In combination with these, if over a period of months you notice that your child displays high levels of persistence, motivation, and single-mindedness when involved in a musical activity, it is wise to speak with professional teachers or music school directors about appropriate programs.

However you begin, it is important to remember that the effort you put into your young child's musical education will not only be a foundation for further musical growth, but will have benefits far beyond music: attentiveness, intellectual curiosity, problem-solving ability, and the seeds of self-discipline.

Select Listening

Adventures in Rhythm with Ella Jenkins by Ella Jenkins

African Playground by Angelique Kidjo, Mahotella Queens, others

Carnival of the Animals by Camille Saint-Saëns

Celebration of Folk Music by Pete Seeger, Woodie Guthrie, others

Choo, Choo Boogaloo by Buckwheat Zydeco

Great Big Fun for the Very Little One by Tom Chapin

Lullaby, A Collection by Bobby McFerrin, Judy Collins, Sweet Honey in the Rock, and others

Mr. Bach Comes to Call; Beethoven Lives Upstairs; Mozart's Magic Fantasy: A Journey Through the Magic Flute; Tchaikovsky Discovers America; other titles. (The Classical Kids series all have companion books and videos.)

The Nutcracker, Swan Lake by Tchaikovsky

Singable Songs for the Very Young; Baby Beluga by Raffi

Books for You and Your Child

Friedman, Carol. *Nicky the Jazz Cat*. New York: Powerhouse Books, 2005. (Companion CD available.)

Greves, Margaret. *The Magic Flute: The Story of Mozart's Opera*. New York: Henry Holt, 1989.

Hayes, Ann. *Meet the Orchestra*. New York: Harcourt, Brace, Jovanovich, 1991.

Kalman, Bobbie. *Musical Instruments from A to Z*. New York: Crabtree Publishing Company, 1997.

Krull, Kathleen. *Gonna Sing My Head Off*. New York: Knopf, 1992.

Kuskin, Karla. *The Philharmonic Gets Dressed.* New York: Harper & Row, 1982.

Moss, Lloyd. *Zin! Zin! Zin! A Violin.* New York: Simon & Schuster, 1995.

Turner, Barrie Carson. *Carnival of the Animals, by Saint-Saëns.* New York: Henry Holt & Company (Book & CD edition), 1999.

Willard, Nancy. *The Sorcerer's Apprentice.* New York: Scholastic, 1993.

Resources

Early Childhood Music and Movement Association
805 Mill Avenue
Snohomish, WA 98290
(360) 568-5635
www.ecmma.org

Kindermusik International
6204 Corporate Park Drive
Browns Summit, NC 27214
(336) 273-3363 and (800) 628-5687
www.kindermusik.com

Music Together
Center for Music and Young Children
66 Witherspoon Street
Princeton, NJ 08542
(800) 728-2692
www.musictogether.com

Yamaha Music Foundation
6600 Orangethorpe Avenue
Buena Park, CA 90622
(800) 722-8856
www.yamaha-mf.or.jp

Method Madness

You want your child to build a long-term involvement with music—you don't want it to be just one of those "shoulds" we impose as parents. Music making is about skill development, but it is also about exploring sound, making beautiful sounds, creating something with other people, and carrying on musical and cultural traditions. Any teaching method you choose should enable your child to experiment and allow his or her own creativity to shine through, and also inspire a connection with the material used.

What is the best way to channel your child's musical interest? Traditional methods of teaching instruments are still the most common, especially among private teachers. These methods often entail teaching children to read music notation early on; the age your child begins studying, as well as the instrument he or she chooses, must be considered carefully. Most community music schools offer traditional one-on-one lessons, as well as various classes for the very young and specialized methods or programs. The early phases of the Dalcroze and Orff Schulwerk approaches, Suzuki training, and the Kodály Method are geared toward preschool and kindergarten children. They involve group classes, offer musical exposure, and provide a great foundation for more traditional studies later on. It is possible to begin any of these methods as late as third or fourth grade, though perhaps not as advantageous as simply starting younger.

Suzuki students can progress through increasingly difficult repertoire all the way through high school, and the Kodály curriculum, as practiced in Hungary where it originated, was also intended to go from kindergarten through twelfth grade. However, the availability of these programs for older students may vary considerably, depending on where you live. Various Suzuki and Kodály teaching methods can be incorporated into lessons given by traditional teachers; for instance, many use the Suzuki violin repertoire books because they are carefully sequenced to develop technique and they include many beautiful pieces for beginners.

Watching a teacher in action can often help you make the most informed choice. It's the perfect opportunity to get a sense of the teacher's personality and methodology and to decide if his or her classroom will provide the best learning situation for your child. Most private teachers will offer a trial lesson, and community music schools often host open houses at the beginning of the school year, where you can obtain firsthand information about programs, meet teachers, and see performances by current students. (See chapter 6 for more information about finding teachers.) In any case, once you've discovered the location of the program of your choice, individual teachers are usually willing to allow you to observe their classes.

Traditional Teaching Today

What is traditional teaching? Mostly, it's a set of guiding principles for one-on-one instruction that stems from Western

European musical performance traditions. Ideally, a teacher creates an individualized plan for each student, tailoring a time-honored beginning classical repertoire to the student's age, experience, and individual rate of progression. One of the biggest differences between traditional teachers and those teaching other methods is that traditionally oriented teachers start instructing their students to learn to read music (musical notation) early on. By contrast, beginning Suzuki students learn phrases, rhythms, and whole pieces by ear after hearing them played repeatedly by the teacher and on recordings; they are not introduced to note reading until the second or third year of study. (However, an exception is made for older beginners, who generally make rapid progress and start reading music sooner.)

In general, students start traditionally oriented private lessons when they are school-age and are already getting comfortable with reading language. The cognitive faculties they are developing that help them decipher assembled symbols and letters may be applied to reading music. Some young students really enjoy the challenge of learning to read music, but for others it can be a slow and extremely frustrating process.

Traditional teachers of all instruments today use an array of materials, but still use conventional studies of scales, arpeggios, and études (such as Hanon and Czerny for piano and Shreidecke for violin). Sensitive teachers will also try to find unusual pieces for their students, expose them to different styles of music, and tap into what they think their students will like instead of following a strict sequence of pieces.

In recent years, there has been a trend in community music schools and studios to offer small group classes or semi-private lessons with two or three students. However, many traditional teachers still prefer one-on-one lessons and believe they are the most beneficial method for reinforcing good technique and giving the student individual attention without distractions. The negative side of this is that many young students are pushed into a one-on-one situation before they are really ready to reap these rewards; a class or group may be more advantageous—and more fun—for many children. Don't hesitate to discuss these options with school and program directors to help determine what might best suit your beginner. Some children take to the routine of private lessons right away and relish the individual attention; others may thrive with the added social value of learning with a friend or being in a small group. There is no right or wrong way to begin studying music; you will know if your child is on the right track if he or she is excited about the lessons and wants to try things out at home.

Larry Malin has been a trumpet teacher, teaching privately and in schools, for more than twenty-five years. He feels there is an added burden on traditional teachers today for several reasons:

First of all, there are not so many instrumental programs in the schools—or even *any* music programs in the schools. And most kids don't listen to classical music or acoustic music. The music you hear on the radio today is really different from the music I used to hear on the radio—kids hardly hear classical music at all unless their parents listen to it. Additionally, there used to be a great concert band tradition in this country, which was a huge outlet for many amateur musicians, and that just doesn't exist anymore.

An even bigger problem is that children are not accustomed to delayed gratification. Now, for example, a child can sit down and compose a piece on a synthesizer or a computer and not know a note of music, whereas it will take weeks and weeks to learn a simple song on the trumpet or clarinet, and that is after spending hours learning how to read the music.

Yet, learning a piece of music on an instrument like the trumpet is empowering for a child. When compared to the little effort it takes to generate programmed sounds from an electronic keyboard, the combined process of getting a big sound, learning to read the music, and making it sound musical is worth all the effort. For some children, it might only take a week or two. But Mr. Malin's point is well taken: since we no longer live in a participatory musical culture, a big part of a music teacher's job—regardless of his or her orientation or methodology—is to introduce a child to the joys of being able to make music.

Methodology: Suzuki, Dalcroze, Orff, and Kodály

The above names have all become more familiar in the last twenty years; what many of us tend to forget is they belonged to real people. Shinichi Suzuki, Émile Jacques Dalcroze, Carl Orff, and Zoltán Kodály were all dedicated musicians, composers, and music educators, whose work had a strong philosophical base. Their methods evolved from their musical activities in their respective countries—Japan, Switzerland, Germany, and Hungary—and from their particular cultures and contexts. Dr. Shinichi Suzuki began his now-famous program in the late 1940s, in a spirit of healing and reinstilling culture in war-torn Japan. The musical training associated with Dalcroze, Orff, and Kodály, fundamentally different in approach and content, are linked together historically through the rise of progressive education in Europe (which was also taking place in the United States) throughout the 1800s.

Dalcroze, who taught in Geneva in the late 1800s, felt that many of his conservatory students were technically proficient but lacked real musical understanding; thus he experimented with a teaching approach that combined movement, rhythm, and improvisation. The twentieth-century Swiss composer-educator Carl Orff also devised an approach (known as Orff Schulwerk) that uses movement as a fundamental building block to musical development, along with rhythm and improvisation. He came up with a set of special instruments, easy to manipulate and tuned to sound well together, to inspire exploration in children. The noted Hungarian composer Zoltán Kodály aspired to establish a high level of music literacy, from which creativity would spring. The Kodály Method was founded in Hungary during the 1940s and '50s with his inspiration and guidance and was utilized in state-run schools throughout the country. In the early 1960s its success attracted international attention and the Kodály Method has since been adapted for use around the world.

Orff Schulwerk and Dalcroze are best described as "approaches"—musical learning processes that use movement, rhythm, and improvisation as key elements. They are not instrumental methods, per se, but can prepare students for instrumental study. Suzuki and Kodály are instrumental methods with specifically sequenced curriculum and repertoire. The Suzuki Method uses instruments, primarily violin and other string instruments. The Kodály method uses the voice as the primary instrument. It introduces musical literacy through sight-singing (solfège), reading, and writing music notation early on.

The originators of these methods and approaches thought deeply about children and music and the way children learn. All shared the idea that learning music is an educational process that can be linked to a child's natural development and believed in the harmonious development of the whole child. Currently, they are all taught widely in the United States, and there are institutes and associations (national and regional) connected with each. Most programs bearing these names attempt to re-create the same fundamental philosophies, techniques, and inspirations as their sources, but the way they are practiced can vary from school to school or from teacher to teacher. It would be a mistake to assume that they are interchangeable or that a technique or lesson plan from one can be patched onto another. Their commonality is that they are ideal for young beginners and enhance any sort of subsequent instrument instruction.

At the heart of Kodály's and Suzuki's philosophy is the belief that learning music is similar to language acquisition. Children develop musicality through a process of immersion (hearing the music they will be learning frequently), imitation (copying what they hear), and re-creation (making the music their own expression), the same way they learn their mother tongue. Both methods emphasize and help develop ear training; children become skilled at hearing, repeating, and internalizing a rhythm, musical intervals, or a phrase, and in the process acquire excellent retention skills. Kodály also believed that children have a musical mother tongue, based on the folk music of their culture or country. This is the music they hear and sing, with all the cadences, rhythms, and articulation that surround them.

The Suzuki Method

"A child's ability to develop is proved by being developed."
—Dr. Shinichi Suzuki

Dr. Shinichi Suzuki (1898–1998) believed that every child can develop musical ability with encouragement, repeated exposure, loving support, and playful stimulation. His method is based on his experience and his conviction that all children have a great capacity and desire to learn. Suzuki toured the United States in 1972, demonstrating his Talent Education Program; interest quickly caught on, and music educators latched onto it. The Suzuki Association of the Americas was soon formed (it includes chapters in Canada, Mexico, and South America), and since then the Suzuki Method, with its combined philosophical and pedagogical approach, has had a huge influence on American musical education. There are Suzuki programs across the country, as well as several noted teacher training institutes and summer programs.

One of the most striking results of the Suzuki boom has been a dramatically increased interest in string playing, resulting in greater numbers of string players in youth orchestras and a variety of string ensembles. The Suzuki Method's essential teaching principles and repertoire have remained consistent, though some aspects might vary among programs or teachers. Teachers can receive certified training for the method (though not all teachers do so).

The so-called Suzuki anthem is "Twinkle, Twinkle Little Star." This song provides a base for the first few months of the method. The simple tune helps children learn how to play on two strings, and its several rhythmic variations teach them about rhythm, bowing technique, and other beginning essentials. Students will then move on to beautiful folk tunes and simple Bach minuets, and eventually to advanced solo and concerto repertoire by Bach, Mozart, Vivaldi, and others.

One of the main attractions of Suzuki training to parents is that it was designed for very young children (beginning as early as age three) playing small-scale violins and cellos. (Another Suzuki influence is the widespread availability and affordability of these instruments.) The method has also been adapted for piano, trumpet, and flute, on normal size instruments, and for guitar, which is available in small sizes.

Typically, the Suzuki student has one private lesson a week and also an ensemble class with other children at the same level. For very young students, private lessons are usually thirty minutes, and so is the class (both increase to forty-five minutes or an hour as the student advances in age and proficiency). The size of the classes can vary widely, depending on the enrollment for a given age group and the particular organization. A beginner ensemble might have twelve three-and four-year-olds, and an intermediate ensemble might have twenty students; other programs might just have a handful of students at any level. The point of the ensemble class is to work on ensemble skills—playing the music together and listening to each other—so class size is not the prime consideration.

Frequent low-key recitals and group performances encourage an ease with playing in front of other people, and the sense, early on, that music is about sharing and creating something beautiful with others. The method relies on ear training, and students repeatedly listen to recordings of pieces they are currently learning and will be learning in the future.

The Suzuki violin method encourages physicality with the instrument before children are allowed to bow on the strings; that is, they practice foot placement, hand placement, and bow manipulation. While children typically start Suzuki lessons around the age of four or five, older children may enjoy the program as well; they usually advance rapidly and catch up with their peers. Reading notation is introduced by the time children are seven or eight, and Suzuki training is sophisticated and challenging enough for students to stay with the program through their teenage years.

But take note: the Suzuki Method requires more hands-on parental involvement than other early music methods, although the degree can vary among Suzuki programs. There is usually a parent orientation class, and for the first few months the parent or caregiver is encouraged to learn violin along with the child. The parent also attends the child's lessons for the first year or two (especially when the child is of preschool age) to carefully observe the teacher. This enables the parent to correct the child's position and to practice with her. Many programs offer parent classes with extra sessions on practicing tips.

Most Suzuki programs make a point of creating opportunities for older students to perform with younger ones, which fosters a sense of community and continuity as well as giving the younger children the thrill of performing at big seasonal concerts.

Key points in the Suzuki Method:

♪ Suzuki is an instrumental method, designed for children age three and older.

♪ It is based on ear training, repetition, and immersion; note reading is introduced later on.

♪ All students follow the same sequence of instruction.

♪ Incremental skill development is accomplished through learning the repertoire.

♪ During the first year or two, parents help with daily practice and correctly guide their child.

♪ It encourages musical discipline early on (one of Suzuki's maxims was, "You don't have to practice on days you don't eat"), with continual positive reinforcement and feedback.

The most frequent criticisms about Suzuki training are that there is not enough emphasis on technique and that the transition to reading music can be frustrating for some children because they have been trained to rely on their ears. There may be some truth to these charges but this largely rests with individual Suzuki centers and teachers. All in all, the Suzuki Method offers an excellent musical foundation.

The Kodály Method

Here comes a bluebird
In through my window
Hey! Diddle um-a
Day, day, day.

In the United States, "Bluebird" is as much an anthem for beginning Kodály students as "Twinkle" is for Suzuki students. In the Kodály Method, folk songs are like seeds, a way to learn specifically about melody and pitch and soon identify the notes and intervals, be able to write them, read them, and transfer that knowledge to other material.

The Hungarian composer/educator Zoltán Kodály (1882–1967) was raised on the opposite side of the world from Shinichi Suzuki, but like Suzuki he believed that since all children are capable of lingual literacy, they are capable of musical literacy. Also like Suzuki, Kodály believed that training a musical ear must begin early, in kindergarten, if not sooner. The Kodály Method evolved from Kodály's philosophy that children inherit a musical mother tongue and their cultural identity through folk music and musical heritage. As such, the human voice is the primary instrument in this method. The students begin singing folk music and gradually are exposed to masterworks by Bach, Mozart, Beethoven, and other classical composers. Ideally, this approach leads to the kind of musical literacy that includes reading and writing music, subsequent instrumental study, music appreciation, and deep comprehension.

Kodály was already a noted composer and music educator when he and Belá Bartók, his fellow countryman and composer, started collecting folk music throughout Hungary

during the early 1900s. In the process, Kodály became determined to restore Hungary's musical birthright; Hungarian folk music, art music, and its conservatories and teaching methods had been dominated by classical Germanic and
Austrian influences for more than two centuries. Kodály was
also appalled at the poor level of musical literacy among students entering the highest level of conservatory; they could
not read or write music adequately and hadn't the faintest
notion of their musical heritage.

Over the next few decades Kodály succeeded at his twofold
mission of giving its music back to the people of Hungary and
raising the level of musical literacy. He wanted to help create
an educational system "that could produce a people to whom
music was not a way to make a living but a way of life."

The Kodály Method evolved in Hungarian schools in the
1940s and '50s. The notion of extramusical benefits were
already studied and appreciated in Hungary. For example,
the idea that studying music can aid in the learning of other
subjects, particularly math, was strongly supported, so promoting a countrywide music education program was part of
the core curriculum. The method is based on a sequential
curriculum for sight singing, a rigorous study of all musical elements—harmony, melody, rhythm—and an intensive
study of classical repertoire as the children progress. It is still
utilized in Hungary, where the curriculum runs from nursery
school and continues through a child's entire education. Musical training is integrated with growing literacy in other subjects. Kodály also composed numerous works for children's
choirs that are still used today.

The success of the Kodály Method attracted great interest
at international music conferences during the mid-1960s and,
soon after, music educators from all over the world came
to Hungary to study what went on at the Singing Primary

Schools. It has since been adapted for use in many countries. Today, a person without a musical education is considered illiterate in Hungary—almost everyone plays an instrument and sings.

Kodály's ideas for teaching music came from observing what children do spontaneously—singing, humming, chanting, and responding rhythmically to the music that is part of their culture. He developed a curriculum that begins with the little melodies and five-note scale children around the world sing in nursery rhymes and chants (such as in "Ring Around the Rosie" and other tunes). Through simple folk songs, children are then introduced to concepts that lead to the ability to read music, sight sing, and fully imagine sound internally, to "think in sound." These skills make studying an instrument far easier when the child finally picks one up.

Key points in the Kodály Method:

♪ Singing is the best foundation for beginning to learn music.

♪ It emphasizes ear training and sight singing.

♪ Folk music is the earliest teaching material, and then there is a gradual shift toward learning about musical masterworks.

♪ Students are taught in group classes or as part of the school curriculum, not in private lessons.

♪ Children learn through movement: they use hand signals to go with each note in the scale, and they move the rest of their bodies in response to music by stepping, marching, skipping, and galloping.

♪ Children learn about the expressive elements of music, which heightens their ability to discriminate what suits the piece best: should it be loud or soft, fast or slow, should the notes be accented, and so forth.

♪ It stresses inner hearing and musical memory (singing
the next phrase silently), so students learn to think in
musical sounds.

♪ The Kodály Method provides a comprehensive musical
foundation and is an excellent supplement to instrumental study.

The Kodály Method has a grade-specific curriculum of
songs, movements, and progressively complex musical concepts. During the first year or two of study, a child will learn
thirty or forty songs. Through them the children learn to
sing on key and clap and move to a rhythm. They will also be
introduced to other fundamentals such as dynamics (playing
loud or soft) and how songs are organized (the difference between verses and choruses). Reading and writing music will
follow from this foundation.

Kodály teachers receive rigorous training, and most enter a Kodály program with a degree in music education. Unlike Suzuki, the method does not require intensive parental
participation, though learning the songs and singing them
with your children is a terrific way to reinforce what they are
learning.

Dalcroze Training

*A group of five- and six-year-olds start their Dalcroze class
sitting in a circle. Their teacher greets them with song, plays
a simple phrase on the piano, and the children move up and
down to the phrase. Second-year Dalcroze students confidently sing "5 4 3 2 1" (sol-fa-mi-re-do) using hand motions for
each part. Then they practice singing a simple pattern that is
the basis for a song they will sing later on in the class. The piano repeats the motif. This is how the children learn to internalize pitch and rhythm, one musical building block at a time.*

> *The teacher improvises a melody based on what they've just sung, and the children dance around in a circle to what she does—shifting from a march-type rhythm to a skipping rhythm. The Dalcroze philosophy is that the children literally embody the music: by singing, moving, and improvising, they are learning accurate pitch, rhythm, dynamics, and expressiveness.*

Émile Jacques Dalcroze (1865–1950) was born in Vienna to Swiss parents and was raised with the latest European trends in progressive education. While still in his teens, he composed many musicals with a group of creative friends who were passionate about the performing arts. He went to Paris in 1884 and studied with the impressionist composers Delibes and Fauré. He soon became an assistant conductor at the opera in Algiers, where his exposure to Arabic music led him to a new world of rhythmic expression. As an educator, Dalcroze began his first professional appointment in 1890 at the Geneva Conservatory. He soon realized that his students there, though technically advanced on their instruments, were not very expressive. Dalcroze dedicated himself to improving this deficiency. He sought to transform the traditional teaching methods of sight singing, rote playing, and learning notation into a basic experience with musical sounds—the felt body, as it were. Dalcroze believed that early instrumental technical training actually impeded musical understanding and expression. He devised exercises that required his students to move freely to different rhythms and pitches and to learn to improvise. He wanted to train them to respond more fully to rhythm and to play with more sensitivity.

Dalcroze eventually came up with a system with three branches: movement in response to rhythm and musical content (called eurhythmics), singing, and improvisation. Today, classes for young students integrate all three with a variety of musical activities. As the students become older and more advanced, the three branches are formally separated, each having its own class. The goal is for them to develop all of the capacities we use when we engage in music: hearing, sight, touch, cognition, and expressiveness. Dalcroze referred to the coordination of these capacities as the *kinesthetic sense*, which can be described as a feedback mechanism that conveys information between the mind and the body. In other words, it's a way to educate the senses.

In the United States, Dalcroze training is mainly offered to preschoolers (the ideal age to begin) and elementary school children; in some (most likely private) schools, the training can continue through middle and high school levels. Dalcroze instructors receive rigorous training that leads to certification; they must be adept themselves in movement studies and be able to improvise on piano to lead their classes.

Virginia Hoge Mead, a prominent Dalcroze educator, wrote that Dalcroze techniques are

> based more on an awareness and understanding of Dalcroze philosophy than on a specific course of action for each age level. Teachers of young children recognize the importance and value of using Dalcroze techniques . . . because the children's world is one of sound making, movement, and play, and the use of their natural behavior ensures learning.

The techniques are not widely used in upper grades, as older students, unless they are also studying dance, tend to be more self-conscious about their bodies and movement. Many children with Dalcroze training go on to study instruments, using the benefits of their training.

The Dalcroze approach was considered radical when it was first introduced, but current research in music education supports Dalcroze's experiential, exploratory approach—one that builds upon a child's natural sense of wonder and joy in movement and sound.

Key points of Dalcroze training:

♪ A pre-instrumental comprehensive approach develops sensitive musicianship.

♪ Students learn to express themselves through listening and movement first, transferring what is deeply felt into voice and instruments later on.

♪ Children learn to make their movements fit the music accurately—in terms of moving to a tempo, using small or large movements, and so forth.

♪ In the second year of study, students start learning to read and write notation through sight singing (solfège).

♪ All styles of music (classical, jazz, folk songs, even popular songs) are used for eurhythmics and improvisation.

♪ Dalcroze training is a foundation for instrumental study and can also act as a complement if the child is doing both at the same time.

The Orff Schulwerk Approach

A group of six- and seven-year-olds are sitting in a circle in a brightly lit room in a community music school. There is a map of Ghana and photographs of master drummers on a bulletin board. A rhythm is written on a music blackboard that would sound like "Slide, two three four, slide, two three four." The children sing an African greeting song and pass a brightly colored egg-shaker around. As they pass it, they shake it to the rhythm on the blackboard: "up and pass, up and pass." They quickly learn the words to the chant and sing as they pass. The teacher then distributes a variety of African percussion instruments—calabash, cabasa, cowbell, clave, log drum, wooden bells—and they play the rhythm. They split into two groups,

players who take a turn with each instrument while singing
and dancers; then the groups switch roles.

Next comes a class of nine- and ten-year-olds. They have
written poems to two figures in Greek myths—Poseidon,
god of the sea, and Artemis, sister of Apollo. After their
greeting song, they choose instruments from an assortment
of wooden and metal xylophones, recorders, rain sticks, and
cymbals. They start setting their words to music. "The sliver
of moon is silvery grey" is now accompanied by the gentle
shaker sound of the rain stick and a low scratchy sound on
the cymbal. Soon the students improvise all together, adding
a repetitive dreamy melody on the xylophone; meanwhile
some of them move to the music.

The children's progression from playing simple rhythms to
creating complex music shows the beauty of the Orff Schulwerk approach. The approach is flexible, not specifically sequenced. Every Orff class has a segment involving movement,
singing, playing instruments, and improvising. The format
stems from Carl Orff's fundamental idea that everyone is
born with the ability to sing and to move.

Carl Orff (1895–1982), was already an established German composer when he started adapting some of Dalcroze's
ideas about movement and music for young adults. He
worked with some pioneers of the European modern dance
movement, and their collaborations led to an approach that
became known as Orff Schulwerk (meaning Orff's teaching
approach and materials). It is now commonly known as the
Orff approach. The school in which he did most of his work,
and the instruments he invented for his program, were all de-
stroyed during World War II. After the war he was persuaded
to present his ideas on Bavarian radio.

Orff believed that all children are musical and can develop
their sense of rhythm, pitch, and musical form. His approach

was originally designed for group classes and was meant to be integrated into a school curriculum, although some private instrumental teachers may also use elements of the Orff approach in their teaching.

Orff invented special instruments that are now widely used in elementary schools and by many music teachers, even if they are not specifically Orff educators. His xylophones and metallophones require no technique; any child can make a pleasing sound with them. They have moveable bars that approximate a five-note pentatonic scale, and almost any combination of these notes sounds good when played together with other instruments. Children also play an array of recorders, wooden flutes, and percussion instruments in Orff classes.

"Process" is a key word in the Orff approach. The elements of music—melody, harmony, rhythm—are explored from their simplest and most elemental forms, and gradually, through more experience, these elements are refined and elevated to complex levels of exploration and music making. Working together in ensembles, students find ways to express themselves musically. They learn through observation and imitation, then experiment and create their own works.

Each class has four elements: a movement piece, a singing piece, an instrumental piece, and a playing piece. Like Dalcroze training, movement and improvisation are fundamental to the Orff process, and children are encouraged to explore sound itself (a dog barking, a door slamming) and experiment with their own voices. Initially children learn folk songs, then gradually use the Orff instruments to play the compositions and arrangements Orff devised for teaching. The Orff approach has been adapted to teach notation, though recognizing melodic contours, patterns, and rhythms is emphasized more than in traditional teaching methods.

Composition is emphasized from early on, and the children are not limited by anything other than their imagination.

Key points of the Orff approach:

♪ Children explore space through movement, sound through voice, and musical expression through improvisation.

♪ Students learn through a gradual process: from imitation to original creations, from simplicity to complexity, from the individual to a group.

♪ Children sing chants, nursery rhymes, and folk songs, and move on to playing percussion instruments and the Orff mallet instruments.

♪ Children learn how to create repeating patterns (think Phillip Glass) as a "seed" for composing.

♪ The Orff approach can be easily integrated with literature and social studies; music is composed for stories, to enact myths and folk tales, and more.

♪ Teachers are trained to recognize different learning styles in children (some learn by ear, others by exploration).

Overall, the fact that the methods discussed here have become familiar and are used in community music schools and in public and private schools alike is a testament to their effectiveness as educational models. Additionally, keyboard classes, along the lines of the Yamaha program, have been adopted for use by many schools as a more conducive way to teach keyboard technique in a motivating social setting. It is also inspiring to find programs developed by musicians themselves. The prominent violinist Midori (now in her thirties, celebrated as a performer since childhood) started Midori & Friends, an outreach program that provides a multiyear comprehensive musical education program for inner-city schools. School-age beginners can benefit from these methods, as discussed in the next chapter, but, as your child develops, it's time to consider additional aspects of his or her musical education.

Select Reading

Choksy, Lois. *The Kodály Method 1.* Third edition. Englewood Cliffs, NJ: Prentice Hall, 1999.

————. *The Kodály Method 2.* Third edition. Englewood Cliffs, NJ: Prentice Hall, 1999.

————. *The Kodály Context: Creating an Environment for Musical Literacy.* Englewood Cliffs, NJ: Prentice Hall, 1981.

Choksy, Lois and Robert M. Abramson, Avon Gillespie, David Woods. *Teaching Music in the Twentieth Century.* Englewood Cliffs, NJ: Prentice-Hall, 1986.

Dale, Monica. *Songs Without Yawns: Music for Teaching Children through Dalcroze Eurhythmics (or any method!).* Ellicott City, MD: MusiKinesis, 2003.

Keller, Wilhelm. *Introduction to Music for Children (Orff): Methodology, Playing the Instruments, Suggestions for Teachers.* New York: Schott, 1974.

Starr, William and Constance Starr. *To Learn with Love: A Companion for Suzuki Parents.* Knoxville, Tennessee: Kingston Ellis Press, 1985.

Suzuki, Shinichi. *Nurtured by Love: The Classic Approach to Talent Education.* Albany, IN: Worldwide Press, 1969.

Warner, Brigitte. *Orff-Schulwerk: Applications for the Classroom.* Englewood Cliffs, NJ: Prentice Hall, 1991.

Zemke, Sister Lorne. *The Kodály Concept: Its History, Philosophy, and Development.* Champaign, IL: Mark Foster, 1981.

Resources

The national organizations listed below have regional and local chapters, with program and teacher referrals.

American Orff-Schulwerk
Association
P.O. Box 391089
Cleveland, OH 44139
(216) 543-5366
www.aosa.org

Dalcroze School of the Lucy
Moses School/Kaufman Center
Anne Farber, Director
129 W. 67th Street
New York, NY 10023
(212) 501-3303
www.kaufmancenter.org

Dalcroze Society of America
This Web site has links to regional and local offices, current research relating to Dalcroze training, programs for students and teacher training, as well as literature and teaching materials.
www.dalcrozeusa.org

Midori & Friends
352 Seventh Avenue
New York, NY 10001
(212) 767-1300
www.Midoriandfriends.org

National Piano Foundation
13140 Coit Road
Suite 320, LB 120
Dallas, TX 75240-5737
(972) 233-9107
www.pianonet.com

Organization of American Kodály Educators
1612 – 29th Avenue South
Moorhead, MN 56560
(218) 227-6253
www.oake.org

Robert Abramson Dalcroze Institute
250 West 94th Street
New York, NY 10025
(212) 866-0105
www.dalcrozeinstitute.com

Suzuki Association of the Americas
P.O. Box 17310
Boulder, CO 80308
(303) 444-0948
www.suzukiassociation.org

Yamaha Music Foundation
6600 Orangethorpe Avenue
Buena Park, CA 90622
(800) 722-8856
www.yamaha-mf.or.jp

Tuning Up

Yu've done some research and found out what types of music programs exist nearby and what some of your friends' school-age children are up to musically. Your child, now in second grade, has been hankering to start an instrument, and you've decided it's time to move forward. This chapter focuses on school-age children (six- to twelve-year-olds) and features additional information for preteens and teens. It addresses the main issues you will be facing, including picking an age-appropriate instrument, a suitable program, and a teacher.

As noted in the previous chapter, there are numerous benefits for children who start music lessons while still in preschool, but there are advantages to starting later, too. School-age children are generally far more physically coordinated. What might be daunting to a four-year-old who requires constant corrections—particularly in terms of positioning the instrument (holding the violin on the shoulder, holding the bow with a certain grip, and so forth)—can come easily to a six-year-old. Elementary school children are capable of comprehending and expressing real musical ideas, such as recognizing melodic themes and compositional forms. Children in

first and second grades are already reading, so they will likely
be able to grasp musical notation, too. And they generally
have a longer attention span than the preschool set.

For school-age children, whether they are kindergartners or approaching middle school, it's important to keep
the big picture in mind. Studying an instrument is an incremental process that engages the body, the intellect, and the
emotions. Acquiring skill on a musical instrument is much
like becoming a good athlete: it takes a willingness to learn
things inch by inch, stick with a challenge, and not get too
upset about making mistakes. Your musical child who sang
all day as a toddler may, a few years later, go through many
frustrating moments at the piano or on the saxophone.
But the inches add up—suddenly things connect and the
achievement of making something sound musical, or of
overcoming passages that at first seemed difficult, becomes
a reward in itself.

Choosing the right instrument and finding the right teacher
are the foremost concerns for beginners of any age (see chapters 5 and 6 for more detailed information). The children in
the younger end of this age group, between five and seven
years old, are still limited to traditional beginners' instruments or to instruments made in small sizes. These include
piano, guitar, violin, cello, and recorder. These instruments

can, of course, be excellent starting instruments for eight- and nine-year-olds as well, but the possibilities for children in this age range can be much broader. They have the option to choose from woodwind (flute, clarinet, alto saxophone), brass (cornet, trumpet, trombone, baritone horn, tuba), and drums and tuned percussion instruments.

Years ago, when elementary school instrumental programs were more common, children typically chose or were assigned an instrument during the third grade and, after a few basic lessons, started playing in the school band. Many instruments were assigned by virtue of a child's size and gender, regardless of his or her interests. For example, the largest instruments—tuba, baritone horn, and trombone—were usually doled out to the largest kids, based on the assumption that they could manage and lug these instruments around better. But this is no longer universally the case.

Fortunately, a child's fascination with or urge to play a specific instrument may come about in unanticipated ways. Extracurricular exposure to or contact with instruments is key to igniting a child's interest—especially since we can no longer count on schools to provide this exposure. Lydia, now a college graduate, heard her first string ensemble in one of the enclosed walkways above the streets of Minneapolis one frigid Saturday when she was four years old. It was a children's performance group, and she was mesmerized by the sight and sound of it. Over the next few months she kept asking to play the violin, and within a year her parents enrolled her in a Suzuki program. Music never became a career path for her, but it remains a large part of her life. She was active in her college orchestra and chamber music program and taught violin to inner-city kids as part of an outreach program. Now in law school, she finds that playing violin helps her defuse stress in her life.

Tamara tried out the French horn after attending a New York Philharmonic concert for schoolchildren, one of the symphony's educational programs. The New York Philharmonic is one of many symphonies that emphasize outreach and educational programs as a way of trying to bridge the gap left by the absence of musical education in schools. In Tamara's case, this effort was a success. She was the only child in her kindergarten class who could make a sound with the beautiful, shiny horn, and she went home asking her parents when she could have one. They wisely answered, "when you are big enough to carry it without hurting yourself." The French horn takes a lot of stamina to play, and the horn, in its case, weighs about twenty pounds. Finally, when she was nine, she was ready. She has been taking lessons ever since and really loves the instrument. She has learned that playing an uncommon instrument like the French horn gives her many opportunities to join ensembles and far less competition than if she played violin or flute.

Chris Jenkins is a violin and viola teacher and performer, and a laureate of the Sphinx Organization, a Detroit-based group dedicated to promoting diversity in the classical music world. He studied violin all through elementary school and, as he went on, he was encouraged to take up viola. Of this transition he says,

> Violas were needed in my school orchestra. Since I had long arms it was suggested that I try it. I stuck with it and learned to love it, and eventually it made sense to specialize. Facility on the viola is more difficult—it is bigger, bulkier, and harder to hold. But I enjoy the parts a lot more.

Jenkins found that since the viola not a commonly studied instrument, viola players are in demand. There are many more opportunities for violists to perform in a variety of groups and achieve recognition than there are for violinists, even at the middle school or high school level. He also found that, generally speaking, viola players were not quite as competitive as violinists—they didn't always need to stand out. This quality is fortunate from a musical point of view, for the role of the viola in classical music is generally to blend its sound with the rest of the string section.

Your child's interest in an instrument may also reflect some personality traits that seem counter to type. The shy child, not the extrovert, may want a loud showy instrument such as drums or trumpet. Or a very active child may want to settle down with a ponderous instrument such as the cello. Professionals have a broad perspective on this, especially those who were coaxed into studying a particular instrument.

Many successful musicians didn't start out on the instruments that are now their specialty. Flutist Paula Robison started unsuccessfully (and unhappily) on piano. To her, the piano was an overwhelming instrument—practicing was a very isolating experience, and it seemed too large and too difficult to master so many keys. Once she discovered the flute, she knew she'd found her perfect match in sound, size, and temperament.

Generally, school-age children should have a big voice in their choice of instruments—and going along with your child's instincts will probably be the best motivation for him or her. Provide support and a good teacher; nurture fascination for the instrument by seeking out CDs or videos that feature it; go to live performances and recitals. Once you finally acquire the chosen instrument, help your child adopt it. Even if it's a rented instrument, it is something special that he should consider his own, to take care of, take pride in, and be able to show off to friends. Be enthusiastic about your child's early efforts, even if squeaky violins and raspy trumpets are painful to listen to at the moment.

Mechanics of Lessons

Music lessons are a collaboration among student, teacher, and parent. The process should be low-key and fun, yet still achieve definable skills over a period of time. Your child may get frustrated and want to quit if progress is too slow or if demands are too great. The first few lessons on any instrument involve multiple sets of physical coordination—how to hold the instrument, sit correctly, get a good sound, and so forth. Don't be shy about asking your child's teacher what will be going on in the first few lessons, how much practicing would be helpful to achieve certain skills early on, and what you can do to help at home to keep things engaging and positive. For example Suzuki teachers encourage—and some programs require—parents to sit quietly at the lesson and take careful notes on such things as correct bow hold, breathing, and posture to ensure that the child will be practicing correctly at home. This is a good idea no matter what method or kind of instruction your child is receiving.

Observing your child's lessons is valuable, both for you and for your child, particularly when your child is first starting out and if you have no musical training yourself. Remember that you are there as a fly on the wall. You want your child to look to the teacher for instruction and guidance, not to you, and you want the two of them to build a good learning relationship. But it's helpful to pull out your notes when your child practices at home and make sure your child is on the right track.

For very young children, the added layer of knowing you are sitting at the lesson can be very comforting and encouraging. Not all children will need that extra layer of support, but most of them will need the additional coaching about how to do something correctly.

Here are some points to bear in mind once your child starts instrument lessons.

♪ For beginners, a weekly thirty-minute private lesson or ensemble class is typical.

♪ One parent should quietly observe the child's lessons, especially if the parents have no musical training themselves.

♪ This parent should take notes during the lesson, paying special attention to instrument position and sound production.

♪ Make sure that you and your child know what to focus on during practice sessions at home and how much time your child should spend practicing specific things. Some teachers write this information down, but not all.

♪ Make up a colorful activity chart to keep track of daily practicing and small achievements.

The one-on-one attention between teacher and child during private lessons can be very rewarding for many children. Like an excellent classroom teacher, a good music teacher should get your child excited about the process. The teacher should be organized and developmental in approach and repertoire, yet still appreciate your child's individual way of processing what is being taught. But above all, a child's first teacher should really enjoy working with young children. According to a survey of professional musicians by Dr. John Sloboda, a British psychologist who has done extensive research on musical achievement, the quality that musicians valued the most in their first teachers was personal warmth.

These teachers may not have been the best performers, but they were friendly and could communicate enthusiasm and their love of music. The same respondents considered their early lessons a highlight of their week, in contrast with the experience of many low achievers in music who dreaded lessons and found them anxiety-provoking and even humiliating. Sloboda suggests that teachers who

> stretch and challenge their pupils to go beyond what is immediately enjoyable and achievable seem to have the greatest effect on students who are already committed to music. The task of the first teacher may be to help develop that love of music which leads to long-term commitment.

How can you tell if this love of music is being nurtured? Pay close attention to what your child says about the teacher and the lessons. Is she excited? Does she say she can't wait to try a new sound or a new piece? That is the kind of feedback that you want to hear.

You want your child to be able to establish a good rapport with the teacher, one that inspires her to do the work of learning to play the instrument. Sensitive teachers will surround their corrections with positive comments and encouragement and will try to inject good humor frequently. A teacher's overemphasis on perfection or rapid achievement during the lessons may be detrimental to a beginner—a child should not feel as if he or she can never do anything right.

Try to get a feel for the music your child is working on. Is it motivating your child's interest? Does he work on particular pieces of music at home with no prompting from you? Does she sing or whistle the music she is studying? Children should like a good portion of the music they're working on, though inevitably they won't care for all of it.

To Read or Not to Read (Music, That Is)

Why learn to read music? Written music is a common language, and the ability to read music gives children a way to learn common repertoire, have a link to a variety of styles, and learn the music of different cultures. Learning to read and write music is a big part of musical literacy, and it can provide opportunities for children later on, such as playing in an advanced-level band, orchestra, or chamber group or composing their own music so that other people can easily play it. Musical notation is the written element of a language that gives everyone access to the same material.

Traditionally oriented teachers and some music methods introduce learning musical notation along with the rudiments of learning instruments. If you are keen on your child learning an instrument in a traditional fashion, you need to be attuned to your child's readiness. Reading music and teaching little fingers to play can prove frustrating for children until they are ready to focus on it. Most four- or five-year-olds can't struggle with learning to read their ABCs and learning rudimentary music notation unless they are especially driven or are fond of decoding activities. But even for preschoolers and pre-kindergartners, much can be done to lay the foundations for reading music. Children can be introduced to musical symbols, whole notes, half notes, and some other basic ideas.

There are advantages to *not* learning musical notation right away. The foremost is that children don't have to struggle with learning musical notation at the same time they are learning the basic mechanics of an instrument. Another advantage is that this is a chance to utilize the way that young children learn language and phrasing and develop their ears. It is far easier for children to learn music in an aural way, which is how we acquire language skills. They learn by soaking up songs, nursery rhymes, and folk music and by mimicking melodies and rhythmic patterns.

One of the fundamental reasons the Suzuki Method has proved so popular and successful is that it is an ear-based method. It takes reading music out of the process until the children are in first or second grade and are well along with their literacy skills in their native language. Similarly, in several musical genres—jazz, folk music, rock 'n' roll, and ethnic music of many cultures—learning songs, compositions, and improvisational idioms is largely, if not completely, an aural tradition. The music is learned by immersion, mimicry, repetition, and modeling, not sheer memorization. Learning to play with expression and nuance are part of this process. The ways in which students develop from ear-based training are wholly individual, but children who learn music in this fashion do more than memorize it—they are learning to internalize it, as well as to develop their ears. Good musicianship relies on keen ears—for playing in tune, with sensitive phrasing and good retention, and for really focusing on the music itself instead of just what's on the page.

On the other hand, well-developed ears among young music students are the bane of many traditionally oriented teachers. The students' heightened facility in learning music by ear often makes them impatient with the process of learning to read music, especially if they are introduced to learning notation at age seven or eight, or in some cases, even older.

"This is my objection to Suzuki," says Felice Swados, who teaches piano and harp.

I had one student who started as a Suzuki violin student. She was eleven and really accomplished, but she couldn't read a note. Her parents wanted her to work with someone more traditional on reading skills. I spent the entire year working with her. She kept saying, "Why don't you just play it for me?" I refused to do it that way, and it was really frustrating for her and for me. Here was this kid who had this fabulously developed ear, and she said, "Why should I waste my time with this?" I just kept telling her if she just worked on it for two weeks she'd be able to do it.

At times, I feel irritated by the Suzuki Method—it's so prevalent. I can understand at three, four, five years old not reading music, but after that! It's like teaching language to people that don't read words. You miss a lot of what this is about.

Most kids with Suzuki training have fantastic ears, which is nothing to sneeze at either. I have college students who come to me and they have never tuned their harps by ear. They don't know how. They all use electronic tuners, which weren't available when I was growing up. So I've spent lessons where I'll say, "Play the fifth, play an octave—hear what it sounds like, does it sound sharp or flat?" They don't have this sense as well developed.

The point is that both sets of skills—a well-developed ear and good reading skills—are important for musical development. Brenda Dillon, project director for the National Piano Foundation, says:

It's really important to give your students the right balance of ear development and reading skills. . . . If one skill gets far ahead of the other skill, there is a problem. Even the best ear players will tell me they wish they could read music better—they feel like they are somewhat crippled. I'm sure given the choice they would prefer to have their good ears above the reading. How many people do you know that can read music—but they don't seem to hear thunder? They haven't developed their ears. If you have the ear, you can focus on the music more. The best teaching I have ever seen is where those two stay in balance.

Current methods for learning to read music and sight-reading run the gamut, from using standard method books that emphasize learning a few notes at a time to utilizing the digital pianos and technology that many piano teachers now have in their studios. Ms. Dillon says she finally developed a successful sight-reading method incorporating technology after many years of

> doing everything possible anyone has ever recommended—not looking at your hands, using a metronome, slowing everything down, using every sight-reading book that existed. Now I use a MIDI disc in combination with a method book that is at a less skilled level than the music the student is working on, and I have the student play to an accompaniment. It's kind of a music-minus-one, and the student has to keep up. It has been really gratifying to get this to work for my students, and they love it.

Good sight-reading skills are aided immeasurably by a well-developed ear because the student can more easily anticipate what the music is *supposed* to sound like. Developing the cognitive skills involved in reading music can be rewarding for children; reading music is a way to explore a wealth of musical material on their own—whether it's a show tune, pop song, or Beethoven sonata. Reading music is actually a set of skills that combines recognizing and anticipating many bits of information simultaneously—pitch, duration, melody, and rhythm—and in the case of piano, reading for two or more parts simultaneously. Eventually, it does become second nature, and many children rise to the challenge and enjoy it.

Rewards and Motivation

Rewards are OK! Studying an instrument is a demanding, challenging process that deserves extra acknowledgment.

Without going overboard or getting into excessive bribing and wheedling, find some small rewards that will do the trick. Stickers, stars, cards with musical instruments or musical symbols, and colorful activity charts work like a charm for many children. You can use them to reward a child for maintaining a good position, practicing the same piece a specific number of times, mastering a difficult section of a tune, or for playing something particularly well. However, it's best to try not to duplicate the same kind of rewards the teacher gives out.

Most eight- and nine-year-olds have outgrown stickers and charts. They are ready for delayed gratification and more sophisticated items: a desired yet still inexpensive toy or some special family privilege in exchange for two or three weeks of good practice. Other attractive rewards can include books or videos about composers, pictures of composers, posters, recordings of music that your child is working on or music by favorite young classical musicians (such as Joshua Bell, Hilary Hahn, Regina Carter, or Sarah Chang).

Taking part in festivals and recitals can also be very motivating. Many community music schools have a sharing hour to promote an informal performing atmosphere. But some children enjoy formal recitals. Lydia, profiled earlier, loved preparing for recitals. "It was so exciting," she said. "I loved performing and getting all dressed up. It was a very big deal for me when I was little. Getting a certain piece ready for a specific date was inspiring. I worked really hard for those recitals."

It can also be motivating to make connections between your child's regular schoolwork and his music lessons, particularly when there is no instrumental program in the school. My son's science teacher invited him to play for the entire second and third grades when they were studying sound and building instruments. This turned out to be a great honor for him and source of pride—the questions just kept coming. Not only that, it inspired some other kids to take instrument lessons.

Going to concerts, especially those featuring exciting young artists, can also be an extremely motivating reward. The concerts presented by From the Top, for example, would fit the bill. From the Top, now in its fourth year, is an organization whose mission is to showcase the talents of outstanding teen and preteen classical performers and, in doing so, promote music education. These one-hour concerts take place in various cities around the country, are taped and then broadcast a few months later. (They can be heard anytime on the show's Web site, listed with other resources at the end of this chapter.) The music is interspersed with witty interviews and skits and guest appearances by youthful world-class musicians such as Joshua Bell and Yo-Yo Ma, who were once in their shoes (in some cases not all that long ago). The audience behaves more like one at a baseball game than at a classical concert, but, through all the banter, kids get to witness other kids playing at a professional level yet talking about what they do in a down-to-earth way.

For many kids, and not just advanced students, summer music camps can be fun—at least as much fun as other kinds of summer camps—and inspiring. Music camps and workshops exist in all parts of the country and are usually open to children age eight and older; some require a parent or guardian for children under sixteen; others are sleepaway music camps. There are programs available for a week or two to the entire summer for all kinds of instruments, musical styles, and student ability. Some take place in unusual settings and offer a non-competitive workshop atmosphere. Students can try out new styles (such as jazz or bluegrass) with a variety of teachers. Meanwhile, they can make new friends with students from different parts of the country. Examples include the Mark O'Connor Fiddle Camp, a weeklong workshop that takes place in a state park outside Nashville, and the Rocky Mountain Fiddle Camp in the wilderness at the edge of Rocky Mountain National Park.

Ann Roberts's twin boys have attended fiddle camp for three years. "It's become a real motivator for them," she says.

> We're around kids who are very, very good, so they can see what's possible and how much work that takes. Plus, they get to hang out with other kids who do what they do. Fiddle camp has really made it rewarding for them. They'll hit lows during the year—but they know that if they quit violin they can't go to fiddle camp, and they don't want to do *that*. Now they talk about getting electric violins and playing in a rock band when they are older, so they are really seeing themselves playing music in the future.

As in other aspects of parenting, the goal is to enable your child to motivate herself. Again, athletics is a good model for what's involved. There is no quick route to becoming adept or accomplishing something that really does take time and practice. Over the years, your child will discover his own way of keeping this adventure in music engaging, fun, and absorbing without you acting as a constant cheerleader.

The Practice of Practicing

Practicing an instrument is very different than playing for fun, merely exploring the instrument, or performing familiar pieces without worrying about glitches or kinks. These are all activities that most children will happily carry out, no coercion necessary. But productive instrumental practice *is* goal oriented. These goals should include problem solving, skill development specific to the instrument, musical understanding, and establishing correct physical habits until they become automatic.

Creating a good practice routine, whether your child is five or fifteen, plays a crucial role in the success of his or her child's musical endeavors. It requires some very grown-up thinking—an intense level of concentration, repetition, and patience, achieving small consistent goals that will have long-term results. Few children *like* to practice, and this fact can cause uproars in otherwise very civilized families. Yet, practicing is essential to making the kind of progress that will fulfill and motivate your child. (Please see chapter 7 for a more detailed discussion of practicing issues and advice.)

Your child is most likely on an enrichment path with music—not a career path—but looking at the practice habits of professionals, or very accomplished students, can be helpful. The Leverhulme Project, a study carried out by Dr. Sloboda in the mid-1980s, found that most young high-achieving musicians practice at least three times as much as less accomplished musicians. Sloboda also found that the most accomplished students were self-motivated to practice (no nudging required!) by the time they were adolescents. This group also had extremely supportive parental involvement in their early years of instrumental study, while the lower-achieving groups were typically told to "just go and practice" by their parents, without daily involvement or active supporting interest.

Developing good practice habits is not just a matter of strong-arming our kids into practicing material they don't like. It's about developing a system, with some flexibility, that mixes up easy pieces, difficult passages, technical exercises, and music your children truly enjoy playing. It takes a certain amount of time to get over progressive humps of technical facility to make music, however easy or difficult the particulars of the instrument. It becomes self-rewarding at different stages, ages, and levels of musical development—and there is always something new to discover.

Ann Roberts and her eleven-year-old twins live in Dallas, a culturally rich city with an acclaimed symphony and a youth symphony, but even Ann admits that studying classical music is foreign to most of her sons' friends.

They started lessons when they were five—we could just see how much they loved music—but they've gone through stages with it. When they were younger, they'd ask, "Why do we do this? None of our other friends do this. We feel like playing, why do we have to stay in and practice?" When their friends came over, they'd hide their violins! It just wasn't cool. And we just told them all along that music is part of their education and that we feel real strongly about it.

I've seen a lot of parents start this and then stop. Some parents are really wimpy, and they don't see the big picture. Of course kids don't like to practice; it's work, and what kid wouldn't rather be out playing with friends? But you can't give in to your kid's inclination to go out and play when he actually enjoys music, and as an adult he is going to really be enriched by his ability to play. You just have to stick with it.

Now they are going to a new school where half of the kids take a music class. And they are with guys who heard them play at an assembly and think it's cool, and they go home and tell their parents they want to play violin. So they are in a more supportive environment. Part of me thinks they started too young—it was hard for them to deal with the frustration of practicing as five-year-olds. But I do think that the years of discipline, and knowing that this was just part of their life, makes it like brushing their teeth. Though they'll skip brushing their teeth, too, sometimes!"

Practicing does not have to be a battle for everyone. And even for those families for whom it is a source of conflict, the battle lines do eventually fade. Your child's years of self-discipline and musical participation and achievement will become second nature in your family's life.

When to Listen to "I Want to Quit"

There may be times when you have to accept your child's reasons for wanting to quit music lessons. At other times, it may be a matter of switching gears, changing teachers—or just letting things go a bit. If somehow, between homework and sports and practicing, things have become too much of a grind for a seven- or eight-year-old, maybe it is time to let your child change his or her routine. See if your child enjoys lessons again if he doesn't practice—or just practices every other day. Don't be shy about talking to your child's teacher about this, and be aware of times when you know your child feels overscheduled or the stress of too much homework. It's OK to ask the teacher to ease up on practice assignments. Music lessons and practicing should not feel like relentless work for a child.

"You have to know when to intervene and when not to," says Felice Swados, a piano and harp teacher.

Sometimes music lessons can be a big burden for children. I have one little boy who I've been teaching for years. He's kind of all over the place—he's borderline ADD and a lot of my work with him has just been getting him to focus. Mostly we do duets together. That's what he seems to thrive on—and I slip in a solo piece here and there. He's now eleven and for the last three years he kept telling me, "I'm going to quit!" And I say, "How come?"

He tells me, "Well, I really don't like music." And I say, "Wow—that's really surprising." He plays with such gusto, he enjoys it so much. He comes roaring into the room and he sits down, stuffs a candy bar in his mouth, and launches into one of the pieces he's learning—and *then* he tells me that he doesn't like music.

Last spring, before the summer break, his mother told me that she didn't want to push him or force him, and she asked me to talk to him about it for next year. So I told him what his mom said, and I told him what I had observed about him. I said, "You just don't act like somebody who doesn't like music. I know there are people that really don't like music, although there aren't very many of them. And there are people that don't like to play, but like to listen to music. I think you are someone who likes to play and likes to listen.

The next fall, he was back. I know that his mom wouldn't have pushed him, and it wasn't about practicing because he didn't practice anyway. So here he is, and now he practices! It's so curious about kids—sometimes all of a sudden they just get all fired up. Maybe he's just maturing.

At times, parents may be sending a message to their children by *not* intervening. Sometimes, especially if you are not observing your child's lessons too often, a teacher may be putting too much pressure on a young child or adhering too strictly to a method that may not be working for a particular child.

For instance, some teachers want their students to perfect a piece before moving on to new repertoire and are sticklers about every technical and musical aspect of the piece. Ann sensed her twin sons' frustration when their violin teacher had them playing the same simple pieces for months, but she was reluctant to intervene with the teacher. In part her reluctance stemmed from the teacher's sterling reputation; she was considered the best string teacher in the area.

Her focus was technical—and this is so important. But for little five- and six-year-old boys, they didn't want to be playing "Go Tell Aunt Rhody" for six months. She needed everything to be perfect before they could move on. They were very quick at memorizing songs, but they didn't have their thumbs in exactly the right place. So they'd fix one thing and something else would go. They got so sick of it. And I didn't blame them—it was such a chore. They really needed to see progress.

My husband and I became so frustrated about the whole process that we finally said to the kids, "OK, you can quit violin." We were so beaten down by the struggle. And they said, "NO! We don't want to quit!" We knew we had to find someone else. They clearly were really interested in music and their violins—and we had to keep that going for them. So we found a new teacher and his attitude was, "If you can't learn something on one song, you can learn it somewhere else." That made so much sense to me—plus he was teaching them tunes that they loved and tying their lessons in with their interests—it really worked out well and really turned them around.

A child who says, "I want to quit" does not necessarily mean it. You have to listen carefully to what has motivated that remark.

Scenario: your son is nine years old, going into fourth grade. He is one of three kids in his class studying violin and playing classical music. With everyone else listening to rap, pop, and hip-hop, you're beginning to worry that peer pressure is kicking in when he says he wants to quit. What do you do?

A few suggestions:

♪ Arrange a time with your child's music or classroom teacher when he can perform in front of the class; the other kids are usually impressed and excited when they see what their classmates are able to do.

♪ Have a music party! Invite friends over—some that play instruments and some that don't. Try to figure out ahead of time some songs the kids can play together.

♪ Set up musical games with friends, such as musical chairs, and have your child perform for the game.

♪ Seek out other young musicians at school to perform together for grandparents, neighborhood events, and so forth.

If your child is persistent about wanting to stop lessons, the process of reassessing progress, motivation, and stylistic concerns is crucial, as is considering switching teachers. By third grade, Danny had more varied musical interests than his Suzuki violin program offered, plus his mother—a musically trained parent—was concerned that his reading ability wasn't progressing very much. She found a more eclectic private teacher—one who could still build on the classical repertoire he'd been learning and was strong on technique, but could introduce some fiddle music and other kinds of repertoire. Danny also was able to join a beginner orchestra. The timing turned out to be perfect. The new approach, new teacher, and being in the orchestra injected excitement into what had become too routine for an energetic boy. The orchestra felt like a sports team—there were kids from all over the city and they were different ages. The conductor was really funny, and the music was not as hard as Danny had thought it would be. The payoff: hearing him brag to his friends about it. Music was "cool" again.

Preteens and Teens: Whose Music Is It, Anyway?

Adolescents undergo all their tumultuous physical, intellectual, emotional, and social change simultaneously. Some crumble with the switch to middle or high school and its increased academic and social pressures; others welcome new and constant challenges and strive, strive, strive. No matter what their attitudes are, music can provide a steadying force for teenagers, a broad channel where they can route their vast energy. Playing music can help them build self-esteem and answer social needs while providing a tool for focusing and concentrating. The intense physical demands of some instruments such as trumpet, trombone, saxophone, and percussion, offer a creative, focused way to expend physical energy. And meanwhile, playing music gives teens an expressive, emotional outlet while they try out new roles and personas.

There is no guarantee that studying an instrument will be a magic bullet for a musical teenager or for the complex problems of inner-city teens. Furthermore, teenagers' desires often outpace their commitment. They can easily underestimate the work it requires to learn an instrument and give up when the going gets tough and the lessons and practicing cut into their social lives.

Yet for some kids, the opportunity and demands can be life-changing.

"Watching my son learn the cello has made me a true believer in the power of studying music," said Marisol, whose son, now in seventh grade, started on cello two years ago through an in-school program taught by Juilliard interns. "He's really changed. He was kind of hyperactive, always getting in trouble for not paying attention. Now he's great. His music teacher is amazed at how far he's come—and she's kept teaching him even after his program through the school ended. He got transferred to a gifted and talented program in his school, he's got a great attention span, people are acknowledging him."

Trumpet teacher Larry Malin, a veteran music educator and performer in New York City, was able to help one of his students pass the stiff audition test for La Guardia High School, a renowned arts high school (the basis for the performing arts high school featured in the movie *Fame*). "Now he is specializing in music and he's really matured. He was a street kid, but I just knew he would flourish if he had the chance. It's not that he plays trumpet as well as the other kids, but it doesn't really matter. He does better in school, he's got a healthy outlook, and he is involved in really positive things."

If your teenager is asking for lessons for the first time and the request is in earnest, these can be very special years for beginning music study. Agree on an adequate trial period and try to clarify goals and expectations with him. Teenagers can learn new skills at lightning speed when it is important to them; they will obsessively practice a song or virtuosic passage to impress their friends.

If your child has already been studying an instrument for a few years, by now he or she should be able to tap into well-ingrained practice habits. But it might be time for new incentives or a new phase of musical exploration. This is when the slowly acquired skills of studying an instrument can really pay off. The self-discipline, good technical foundation, and general musicianship that older children have acquired are easily transferable to jazz, pop, or rock—whatever their favorite music happens to be. Exploring other styles of music or picking up a second instrument can be enticing for teens and can help head off the "I want to quit" mentality that can be particularly acute in these years.

Digital pianos, programmable synthesizers, keyboards, and electric guitars, which teenagers frequently hear in pop music, advertisements, sound tracks, and other contemporary works, can be very appealing instruments for late starters and teens. Many electronic instruments are equipped with pre-programmed rhythmic accompaniment or digital recording capabilities and can be used interactively with home computers. Such instruments can be great tools for exploring composition and arranging and are an attractive complement to studying traditional instruments.

Meanwhile, listen to their music; don't let the procession of new-found bands and CDs go by without identifying one whose music you can relate to. Hold up some artists as examples of rock virtuosity; they might inspire your child to practice her scales a little harder or work on technique.

Selected Listening

Louis Armstrong: *The Hot Fives and Sevens*
J. S. Bach: *Unaccompanied Cello Suites* and *Brandenberg Concertos*
The Beatles: *Meet the Beatles* and *Beatles '65*
Ludwig van Beethoven: *Symphonies Nos. 6 and 7*

Leonard Bernstein: *West Side Story*

Aaron Copland: *Appalachian Spring* and *Billy the Kid*

Paul Dukas: *The Sorcerer's Apprentice*

Duke Ellington: "Take the 'A' Train," "Happy Go Lucky Local," *The Nutcracker*, and *The Queen's Suite*

George Gershwin: *Rhapsody in Blue* and *Porgy and Bess*

Edvard Grieg: *Peer Gynt Suite*

Wolfgang A. Mozart: *Eine Kleine Nachtmusik, The Magic Flute*, and *Rondo alla Turca*

Igor Stravinsky: *Firebird* and *Petrushka*

Peter Tchaikovsky: *1812 Overture* and *Serenade for Strings*

Antonio Vivaldi: *The Four Seasons*

Selected Reading

Ganeri, Anita. *The Young Person's Guide to the Orchestra*. Book and CD-ROM. Narrated by Ben Kingsley, music composed by Benjamin Britten. London: Chrysalis Children's Books, 1996.

Kalman, Bobbie. *Musical Instruments from A to Z*. New York: Crabtree, 1997.

Krull, Kathleen. *Lives of the Musicians: Good Times, Bad Times (and What the Neighbors Thought)*. San Diego: Harcourt, Brace, Jovanovich, 1993.

Levine, Robert. *Story of the Orchestra: Listen While You Learn About the Instruments, the Music, and the Composers Who Wrote the Music!* Book & CD-ROM. New York: Black Dog & Leventhal, 2000.

Ryan, Pam Munoz. *When Marian Sang: The True Recital of Marian Anderson*. New York: Scholastic, 2002.

Siberall, Anne. *Bravo! Brava! A Night at the Opera: Behind the Scenes with Composers, Cast, and Crew*. New York: Oxford University Press, 2001.

Resources

Directory of Youth
Orchestras on the Web
Hosted by the Metropolitan
Youth Symphony,
Portland, Oregon, USA
www.metroyouthsymphony.org
Web links to over 100 American and international youth
orchestras; includes links to
several noteworthy summer
music camps and programs.

From the Top
295 Huntington Avenue,
Suite 201
Boston, MA 02115
(617) 437-0707
www.fromthetop.org
Non-profit organization that
hosts a weekly radio show of
America's top young classical
musicians, taped in concert
in various U.S. cities. Also
promotes mentor relationships
with its featured artists, and
sponsors other innovative educational programs.

Jazz at Lincoln Center
Education Department
33 West 60th Street, 11th Floor
New York, New York 10023
(212) 258-9800
www.jalc.org
Excellent resource for information about jazz history; includes
online jazz curriculum.

Mark O'Connor
Fiddle Camps
Montgomery Bell State Park
Nashville, Tennessee
www.markoconnor.com/fiddle.
camp

Rocky Mountain Fiddle Camp
Mark Luther, Director
4785 East Amherst Avenue
Denver, CO 80222
(303) 753-6870
www.RMFiddle.com

4

Choosing the Right Instrument

Kyoko, an eight-year-old girl with tiny hands, holds an oboe. She stretches her fingers along its key pads and, after a few squeaky tries, manages to get a pleasing reedy sound. A smile spreads across her face as she finally lets out a breath. Khalil, a tall ten-year-old boy, gingerly picks up a trombone. The instructor gives him a few pointers about blowing into the mouthpiece and Khalil soon gets a nice round-sounding note, checks out the slide mechanism, and manages to play a facsimile of a scale. Four girls sit patiently with half-sized violins on their laps; the teacher goes to each in turn, placing the small instruments on their shoulders, showing them where the violin should be ("as if your shoulder was a table") and how to hold the bow.

These snapshots occurred at an instrument open house, an annual event sponsored by the Interschool Orchestras of New York (ISO) as part of its outreach program. The ISO runs a multilevel orchestral program for children from elementary, middle, and high schools, and the open house takes place in a few classrooms in a public high school where the ISO senior-level orchestra rehearses. Each room features instruments from the basic instrumental families—woodwinds, brass, strings, and percussion—and a patient, friendly instructor or two for each group. Kyoko had the oboe coach to herself for a good half hour, as no one else was interested in that instrument while she was there, but children were lined up for a turn on trumpet, trombone, French horn, percussion instruments, flute, and violin.

But whether the children have five minutes or thirty minutes on an instrument, these introductions can work magic by triggering a child's desire to play a specific instrument and to study music. Many communities offer similar instrument tryouts in schools, music schools, libraries, and at family concerts presented by symphonies across the country. Since many elementary schools no longer provide instrumental programs, this may be the first opportunity that children have to handle a musical instrument of any kind.

Thirty or forty years ago, a child typically would arrive home from school one day with a flute or a trumpet—and everyone's music education would begin! Another sad result of the widespread loss of instrumental music programs in the schools is that many parents, as well as their children, no longer have a basic familiarity with musical instruments. This chapter is an introduction to the variety of instruments to choose from and addresses important factors to consider when you and your child are exploring choices. Your child's choice of instrument will also influence how you go about finding a teacher. (You'll find detailed information on specific instruments in chapter 5 and on finding and selected an appropriate instructor in chapter 6.)

The Families of the Orchestra

Understanding some basics about the variety of instruments and the appropriate ages to begin studying them may help lead you and your child to the right choice.

Orchestral instruments are grouped in four main families—strings, woodwinds, brass, and percussion—by the kind of sound, the way you make the sound, what they look like, what they are made of, and history (for instance, flutes are still woodwinds even though they are now made of metal). The strings produce a sound when you bow or pluck the strings; woodwinds are instruments you blow into or across, and some produce sound with a vibrating reed attached to the mouthpiece; brass instruments are played by forcing a column of air through a cup-shaped mouthpiece; and the huge family of percussion instruments are rung or struck with mallets, sticks, and other implements. Additionally, keyboard instruments (piano, organ, harpsichord) and instruments such as guitar and harp can be played as solo stand-alone instruments or as part of an ensemble.

Whether or not you have experience with musical instruments, ask yourself what kind of activity your child will enjoy. Does he like to blow through tubes? Make soft sounds or enormously powerful ones? Does your child like the feel of wood or metal? Is this a kid who loves banging on pots and pans? Will playing a particular instrument charge your child's curiosity or challenge her to want to master the mechanics of key pads? Does it have a sound your child likes to hear or to make? Is the instrument pleasing to hold? How does fascination for an instrument begin?

Ariel, now an advanced thirteen-year-old violinist in a prestigious conservatory preparatory program, wanted to play violin after hearing a teenage girl play for her preschool class. Zachary, who came from a family where no one ever played an instrument, was inspired to start studying the saxophone after watching a classmate perform at various school functions. Celeste, a fifteen-year-old flute player who never managed to play first chair in her youth orchestra, decided to pick up bassoon because the orchestra needed it. She fell in love with the instrument, which is far more difficult to play than the flute but gives her more performance opportunities where she can really stand out.

These are a few examples of the factors that can influence a child's attraction to an instrument. Some children fall in love with the way an instrument looks or sounds; some have an affinity for a certain physical sensation—the feel of wood or metal. Some children are inspired by seeing their friends perform and watching them play more exciting music as they advance. Others change instruments to give themselves more opportunities.

Children can also reveal a healthy competitive streak or a bit of show-off mentality. When Tamara, now thirteen, discovered at the age of four that she could get a sound out of the French horn, she was thrilled. That thrill has stayed with her even though she did not start taking lessons until she could carry the horn comfortably at age nine:

After I finally got the horn—for a while I just practiced on a mouthpiece—it was kind of like "Look! I can play this!" And my friends said, "OK—you've showed us ten times already!" And then I'd say, "But you can't even get a sound out of it!" My dad still can't get a sound out of it. It was literally—I'm going to call it a gift. I mean, piano is different—you press the keys. But this is something that actually needs stamina and good breath to play—and I have it! That's really hard to get naturally.

Tamara made the right choice, one that has been long-lasting. She is still in love with the sound and feel of her instrument. She also clearly relishes advancing in the citywide orchestra and participating in special school functions that have arisen as a result of her choice.

Chris Jenkins, a professional violist and teacher who also has a degree in psychology, believes—as do many musicians—that there are some psychological elements that affect people's choices, as well as other personality traits that become apparent when you've been playing the instrument for a few years. "It takes really different personalities to play different instruments—specific personalities develop or are attracted to certain instruments in the first place," Chris explains.

Violinists tend to be very ego-driven—very aggressive and competitive. They have to be, there are so many of them! Violists tend to be more easygoing, friendlier to each other and to the other instrumentalists. At music schools, violists tend to form a friendly little clique, while violinists tend not to hang out with anyone. Pianists are the worst, of course—they don't spend time with anyone but themselves.

Additionally, there may be some cultural and gender factors shaping children's choices or interests. For example, a recent study of more than six hundred kindergartners and fourth graders used eight instruments that adults typically classify by gender—with flute, violin, clarinet, and cello classified as feminine and drums, saxophone, trumpet, and trombone as masculine—to see if these classifications held true for children, too.

The children were broken into groups that watched three different videos of high school instrumentalists playing the same piece of music: one showed the performers playing on the typically classified instruments; the second video obscured the performers, so it was hard to tell who was playing what instrument; the third showed performers on instruments viewed as atypical in terms of the musician's gender (that is, girls playing trumpets and saxophones, boys playing flutes, violins, and cellos). The researchers found that the majority of the kindergartners' choices conformed to the stereotypical gender classifications of instrumental choices. However, after viewing the counter-stereotype video, the kindergartners of both sexes and the fourth-grade girls were then more open-minded about what instruments they would choose to study. "These kinds of choices and stereotypes can affect what you learn and what you do later in life," said Betty Repacholi, the study's author.

> A little boy may be the next Yo-Yo Ma, but is not encouraged to play the cello. So he picks the drums, is terrible, and winds up not playing any musical instrument. Or a girl who wants to play the trombone is advised not to, and that stops her from pursuing a career playing that instrument. We need to present both males and females playing a full range of instruments to show that anyone can play them. Gender should not be relevant.

Repacholi's aim, in part, was to show that stereotypes affect all kinds of activities, including the sports people play and their career choices. It is interesting to note, however, that many acclaimed professional musicians counter stereotypic notions of gender-associated instruments, as well as racial and cultural stereotypes—notably, the cellist Yo-Yo Ma, flutist James Galway, percussionist Evelyn Glennie, and violinist Regina Carter, among others. Helping children view such musicians as role models can show our children the full range of possibilities open to them.

Making Choices

Age, physical size, and small- and large-motor coordination are huge factors in helping your child choose the right instrument. For very young children, it will ultimately be your choice—but even so, there are several things to consider. Until fairly recently a piano was a fixture in many people's homes (decades ago, it was *the* entertainment center), and therefore was the obvious choice for a starting instrument. For many of us, it still is—one can easily produce pretty sounds and pick out melodies, and all the notes are laid out logically. Violins and cellos are available in sizes small enough for three-year-olds, and there are also small-size classical guitars. Five- and six-year-olds can have fun with recorders, which make excellent starter instruments. Some woodwinds (clarinet, flute, and alto saxophone) and brass instruments (cornet, trumpet, euphonium, and baritone horn) are more appropriate for eight- to ten-year-olds; they are not made in small sizes and they require good coordination, breath control, strength, and stamina.

As parents, we may end up discouraging our child's choice of musical instruments for our own reasons—how noisy a trumpet or set of drums is, for instance, or how cumbersome it is to get a string bass to lessons or school. But if a child shows a sustained, passionate interest in a specific instrument, it is usually wise to follow that interest.

Eve Weiss, a classical guitar teacher whose son is an accomplished ten-year-old jazz violin player, knows this firsthand. She suggests that

> if you have a kid who expresses a desire for an instrument very strongly, that's what you should go for. If not, you pick the instrument—or you help guide them toward a choice. I advise parents to go see instruments with their kids and get videos of people playing them—cello, guitar, violin. I have one student named Peter who started on piano, but it wasn't a good match. I think he really didn't want to play the piano. But he's a friend of my son and saw kids traipsing in and out of here for guitar lessons. Last year he said he wanted to play the guitar and have me teach him—it's been wonderful. He just loves the guitar.

Children have their own instincts and vision that do not always conform to ours. Switching instruments can be the right choice if the child displays the interest and enthusiasm.

Following your child's interest in an instrument can help her stay committed to her vision of herself making music on that instrument and will help her enjoy the process. She will need to sustain her musical vision for years to come—through the ups and downs of practicing while attempting to achieve a level of virtuosity that satisfies her.

Some of the less commonly chosen instruments, such as oboe, bassoon, French horn, or harp, are more suitable for children nine and up. The technical demands of these instruments, including firm muscle control and coordination, stamina, and the ability to sustain the weight of the instrument in a certain position, are greater than for other instruments. Younger children are often attracted to such instruments, thanks to the sound and uniqueness of each. In this case, it would be a good idea to play a simpler instrument or take a general music class to sustain their interest until they are physically ready.

"Harp is not a good instrument as a starter," says Ms. Swados, a piano and harp teacher. "When parents call me and tell me their six-year-old wants to play harp, I advise them to start on piano or come back in three years. Nine is a good starting age, even though there are small harps. The harp takes a lot of coordination, and there is a lot of technique involved. There is so much to think about without even playing a note."

Some children find themselves falling in love with an instrument because they now have the access to it. (This is another strong reason to fight to bring back instrumental programs in schools.) Larry Malin teaches a band program in an inner-city middle school, where his band class is a requirement. Several of his students are inclusion students, some of whom have behavior problems and various degrees of learning disorders.

> Some of the kids get really attracted to certain instruments, like shiny trumpets. Very often, it's a feeling they have— "Let me try this." This is a great opportunity for them to do something new. I have a girl in my eighth grade class. Everybody can be running around misbehaving, and there she is practicing her trumpet, trying to figure out what I've been teaching while no one else is listening. It's so important, as a parent, to tap into the hidden resources that your kids have—their talent or affection for certain things. If you see it, you've got to build on that.

The Piano

The piano is a special case, for many reasons. It is the easiest instrument to get a pleasing sound out of with minimal or no technique. It is the most familiar and inviting instrument—

hardly anyone can pass by a piano without trying to pick out a familiar song. And it is the easiest and most practical instrument on which to learn about chord structure and harmony.

Yet the piano also has special pitfalls. It is difficult to fully master this instrument's technique and advanced repertoire. Because of its logical note layout and pleasing sounds, parents are less likely to participate in their children's piano study than, say, violin—an instrument that requires such precision in technique and body positioning that teachers often insist parents supervise their children's practice sessions with great vigilance. Still another problem is that many people start their children's lessons on small electric keyboards nowadays, which do not have the tone, touch sensitivity, and complex sound of an acoustic instrument, and many of them do not have a full complement of eighty-eight keys. This can create a problem for both student and teacher if the student is to progress.

For all the pros and cons, there are arguably more children who take piano lessons than any other instrument lessons, and there are also more children who quit taking piano lessons!

"There are very few children who opt to take piano lessons," says Ms. Swados. "That doesn't mean that they don't like it. But most of the children who take piano lessons do so because their parents want them to. They are not nearly as self-motivated as my harp students, which can be a frustrating experience for a piano teacher."

Brenda Dillon, the education director for the National Piano Foundation and a long-time piano teacher, finds it ironic that "the same parents who hated their piano lessons and begged to quit make their children take piano lessons. Now honestly, parents would never frame it in those words, and yet—why would you make your child do the very same thing that you hated and quit?"

They do it for the very same reasons that generations of parents thought the piano was the ideal instrument for a child to learn: the piano is the one instrument that requires no technique to get a pleasing sound out of and is a wonderful instrument for learning about melody, accompaniment, harmony, rhythm, and orchestration.

Yet it is still a struggle. "Piano might be the loneliest thing a child ever does," Ms. Dillon explains. "When you think about soccer or other sports, or dance—nothing else is taught alone, really—except when it comes to a kid alone taking piano. The ideal would be to have a group class and a private lesson, which is the most perfect setup."

Her view, and that of many other piano teachers, is that "piano education can be broadened to give students lifetime musical skills, not just a handful of recital pieces. The people who still play the piano as adults—and enjoy doing so—are those who can improvise a bit, sight-read, and transpose, but I don't think teachers spend much time on those things. Yet the irony is that the people who still play the piano as adults, and really enjoy it, are the ones who have those skills."

Like the violin, teaching methods and pedagogy for the piano have advanced considerably in the last two decades. Group keyboard classes and programs such as Suzuki piano add a social element that can benefit young children just learning to play.

Preschoolers and Kindergartners

Recognizing Readiness

Don't rush your child. Try to make an honest assessment of your child's readiness to learn an instrument, especially if he or she is very young (between the ages of three and six). The following clues indicate a strong enough affinity and curiosity for music to begin the process.

Your child

- ♪ enjoys listening to music and responds with movement or sings along

- ♪ has favorite recordings or pieces and wants to hear them frequently

- ♪ recognizes familiar music or themes and sings along, mimics them, or completes a phrase if you start it

- ♪ recognizes the sound of different instruments

- ♪ is insistent about wanting to play a certain instrument and repeats this desire for months or even years

Learning Readiness

Make sure your child is prepared in other ways, too. Some aspects of readiness have to do with socialization—a child's willingness to cooperate and pay attention in a group setting. Also, children develop cognitive skills at individual rates, which will affect their readiness for the kind of tasks one encounters in music classes geared for preschoolers.

Your child

- ♪ can read and write and enjoys symbol recognition (even though these skills are not necessary for starting Suzuki)

- ♪ takes pride in learning new things

- ♪ is interested in completing tasks

- ♪ has spare mental energy or attention for a demanding new activity (beyond schoolwork, sports, and other commitments)

- ♪ has time to dedicate to working on music daily

Physical Readiness in Both Age and Size

Age and size are important factors, so be judicious about choosing an age-appropriate instrument for your child to start out on. Your child should be able to hold or reach the instrument comfortably, without straining.

♪ Most children will show an eagerness about a specific instrument or at least a preference for the method of sound production (blowing, plucking, striking). Try to follow your child's interest.

♪ Playing an instrument helps develop coordination and motor skills, but don't overtax your child's physical abilities.

♪ Don't frustrate your child with tasks he or she clearly can't do yet (fingering the strings, holding the instrument correctly). It is better to wait a few months, or even a couple of years, until your child has better coordination and dexterity.

Advantages of Starting Between Ages Six and Ten

Once children are around six years old and older, they are generally stronger and have fairly well-developed coordination and motor skills. By this age your child should have a good amount of exposure to music, which can really kindle the interest to start studying an instrument.

School-age children from six to ten years old

♪ can be more confident about their choices of instruments, as they have had more exposure (hopefully!)

♪ may start on woodwinds (such as clarinet and flute) and brass (such as cornet, euphonium, and possibly trumpet) by the age of eight or nine

♪ can participate in beginning band or orchestra

♪ can participate in decisions about how, what, and when to practice

♪ can be more independent about practicing and lessons by third grade

♪ are mature enough to take pride in their new commitment

Starting as a Preteen or Teenager

It's never too late to start an instrument! Children in this age range are usually self-motivated to select an instrument, rather than having their parents make the decision for them.

In fact, there are some advantages to being an older beginner:

♪ It's an appropriate age range to start your child on the larger and heavier brass and woodwinds, such as tenor or baritone saxophone, trombone, and tuba.

♪ Older students have the multiple physical coordination and cognitive skills to make rapid progress.

♪ Positive peer influences can be motivating! Students can impress their friends with newly won skills on guitar, saxophone, and drums.

♪ Less commonly chosen instruments, such as French horn, oboe, bassoon, or viola, are more appropriate choices for this age range due to size considerations; these instruments can also give students more playing opportunities.

This last idea has actually sparked interest from many quarters, and "endangered instruments" programs have begun to spring up in various parts of the country. This is in response to an awareness among orchestra leaders at all levels—including youth orchestras—that fewer students are playing these instruments, which remain vital to orchestras, chamber groups, and jazz ensembles. In 1990, the Seattle Youth Symphony started an endangered instruments pilot program. The aim was twofold: to help restart instrumental training in middle schools that no longer provided it and to use instruments that are no longer commonly taught, but are still needed in orchestras. The program has succeeded and has spread in various forms to other youth orchestras, as well as to community music schools and other organizations around the country.

Such programs are terrific opportunities for teens. They have a built-in you-are-needed aspect, as well as a you-are-different appeal. Add to that the fact that bassoonists or French horn players are virtually guaranteed a spot in any school band or orchestra, instead of having to compete for spots with scores of flutists and clarinetists, and this might be the right combination of factors to foster your child's interests in these instruments.

Whatever age your child begins, discuss with the teacher how to best build good technique without straining his young body. Be aware of what the correct position is, what causes the least amount of stress to the neck or back muscles, and how to avoid injuries from repetitive movement.

For many young students, the novelty of having an instrument is exciting in itself and inspires them to practice. Small-group study on violin, piano, or guitar can be a good choice for young beginners and very sociable children (and will also be less expensive). Keep reminding yourself and your children that all musical instruments are special. It can take years to develop good technique on some, such as violin or oboe, but all certainly have their challenges. Encourage your children to treat their instruments with care and respect, but remind them that these friendly, usable objects will make music an integral, enriching part of your family's life.

What About Your Readiness?

Learning an instrument is a slow, incremental experience. It requires a lot of enthusiasm and support from the family and a willingness to enjoy the process, which at times can be frustrating. So if your child is showing interest, excitement, and is ready to begin, what about you?

Can you learn enough on an instrument yourself to correct technical errors and position problems? Add another demanding daily activity to your family routine? Listen to the same piece of music many times, not to mention scales and exercises? Is a tuba too big for your daughter to take on the school bus? Is there a place at home where your child can practice comfortably without getting disrupted and without disturbing the neighbors? Can you be as gung-ho about musical activities, such as seeking out concerts and recordings, as you would about cheering your kid at a Little League game?

As parents, we need to keep the creative and joyful aspects of studying music in the forefront. And our own personal history with music, successful or not, may make us push our children too hard, or not hard enough. Music lessons shouldn't feel like one more activity to squeeze in, and practicing shouldn't feel like one more chore. If we can help guide our children with love, good humor, and a sense of discovery, they will find their own experience with music, as well as their own best path to learning. Some, like Ariel, may take to learning an instrument with a complete passion—they can't be torn away from it. For other children, no matter how much they love music, the routines of lessons and practicing may be a struggle, yet their musicality will emerge, remarkably, at a recital, at home, or while playing music with friends or a teacher.

One mother, a veteran of high-pitched practicing battles with her accomplished son, said:

> I think what's most important for parents to try and figure out is whose dream is it, anyway? Do parents want their child to become a musician because for whatever reason, they did not succeed at being musicians themselves—and now want to fulfill this dream through their child? That's not a valid reason, in my opinion, for fighting the big fight.
>
> Or perhaps it's the parents' dream that becoming a musician will become the child's dream. If so, it's still the parents' dream. . . . But isn't it a parent's job to give her kids the tools they need to make their dreams come true? And what if the child doesn't yet know it's his dream?
>
> Our teacher told us of a boy she knows who fought and fought until about age sixteen, when he woke up (from his adolescent stupor perhaps?) and realized that, after all, he loved the violin. There were no issues after that. That's the kind of thinking that keeps me in it.

At one From the Top concert, the renowned violinist Joshua Bell was the featured guest, appearing in his usual T-shirt and jeans. After he performed, he spoke of the home environment that had fostered his talent and of his teacher, Josef Gingold, who had come from a lineage of great violinists. Gingold was "wary of pushy parents," Bell told his young audience. "But you have to have them," he concluded lovingly.

Practical and Financial Concerns

One crucial matter that will also affect your decision about when your child should start taking lessons, and the choice of instrument, is your budget. Can you afford a year of private lessons or fees for two semesters at your neighborhood community music school? Can you afford to buy or rent a piano for your child to practice on? What about a flute? For many of us, such questions can indeed make or break the issue of starting music lessons at all.

The following two chapters include specific information on instrument rentals and purchases, lesson fees, and average costs for sheet music, music books, and incidentals, all of which indeed add up. But bear in mind that lesson fees and instrument rental fees vary considerably in different parts of the country. For instance, in large metropolitan areas such as New York City, Boston, and San Francisco, the average fee is thirty dollars for a thirty-minute private lesson and forty-five dollars for forty-five minutes; in smaller cities and regions, private lessons average fifteen to twenty dollars for a thirty-minute lesson and thirty dollars for forty-five minutes.

Not every family is prepared to spend hundreds of dollars a year to start their four-year-old on violin or piano, or even their six-year-old. But if your child is indeed serious about learning an instrument, most community music schools and preparatory programs offer financial aid, scholarships, and instrument loans to deserving students. Additionally, regional symphonies and chamber groups have made serious inroads into their constituent communities in terms of outreach programs, many of which include instrument instruction. Investigate what's going on in your community for these resources. (Also see chapter 8 for more information about outreach programs.) To find out about the best (and most economical) places to buy or rent instruments in your area, ask for assistance from experienced instrument teachers or veteran parents beforehand. The first question you should ask your child's music teacher is what quality of instrument your child should start out on, keeping your budget in mind. He or she should be able to give information about the differences in instruments from various manufacturers, what to look out for, and what may work best for your child. Music studios or stores that rent or sell instruments will allow you to exchange an instrument if your child's teacher finds it inadequate or substandard. Some stores offer trial or checkout periods of time.

Renting an instrument has many advantages. First, it gives you the opportunity to see if your child will really continue after the first few months before committing to ownership. Second, most student instrument rentals are not costly. For stringed instruments and common woodwind and brass instruments such as flute, clarinet, and trumpet, rental fees plus insurance run approximately $125–175 a year. Piano rentals are typically between fifty and sixty dollars per month, as are rentals for other large instruments such as harp, tympani, xylophone, vibraphone, and marimba. Many music stores have plans for instrument rentals with an option to purchase after several months, which is worth considering once your child has settled into his or her choice of instrument. Some music schools operate their own instrument exchanges; these are particularly useful for small-scale instruments, as children progress through instrument sizes at varying rates.

The purchase of a high-quality instrument is an investment you may not want to make early on. On the other hand, starting out on a poor-quality instrument, whether for convenience or economy, can hamper a student just starting out. Several reliable instrument manufacturers (Selmer, Conn, and Bach) make separate lines of instruments: for students, those looking for an instrument with a mid-range price, and professional quality instruments. (See chapter 5 for average prices, as well as recommended ages for starting.) Student instruments are authentic instruments that are the same size, have the same number of keys and functions as the higher-quality instruments, but are made of less expensive materials (for example, plastic instead of wood for clarinets). Depending on the make, such instruments can be satisfying to play for years.

Unless you have an expert with you, beware of bargains—really cheap or used instruments. They can be difficult to play or keep in tune, and they may require costly repairs. If it is difficult to produce a decent sound on the instrument, it will not be inspiring, especially for a beginner, to play or practice on. It is to your advantage to give your child a decent-quality instrument from the start. Producing a good sound is inspiring and should not be a struggle—it should make a child want to play his or her instrument even more. Additionally, good-quality instruments that are well-cared for never lose their value, and can easily be resold.

Selected Artists

The following musicians are recognized masters on their instruments; some, such as Louis Armstrong, Miles Davis, Dizzy Gillespie, and Vladimir Horowitz, were legends in their own time. Your child may be inspired by listening to their recordings and finding out more about them.

Woodwinds

Clarinet: Don Byron, Benny Goodman, Woody Herman, Richard Stoltzman

Flute: James Galway, Jean-Pierre Rampal, Paula Robison

Recorder: Michala Petri

Saxophone: John Coltrane, Joe Lovano, Charlie Parker, Joshua Redman, Sonny Rollins.

Brass

Trumpet: Maurice Andre, Louis Armstrong, Miles Davis, Dizzy Gillespie, Wynton Marsalis

Trombone: Ray Anderson, Slide Hampton, Jack Teagarden

Brass Ensembles: Canadian Brass Quintet, Dirty Dozen Brass Band, Rebirth Brass Band

Strings

Violin: Darrol Anger, Joshua Bell, Regina Carter, Sarah Chang, Hilary Hahn, Midori, Mark O'Connor, and Gil Shaham

Cello: Matt Haimovitz and Yo-Yo Ma

Chamber Groups: Eroica Trio and Pacifica Quartet

Piano

Emanuel Ax, Jonathan Biss, Duke Ellington, Vladimir Horowitz, Evgeny Kissin, Oscar Peterson, Mitsuko Uchida

Percussion

Cyro Baptista and Evelyn Glennie

(5)

The Instruments

There are few objects as inviting, magical, and historic as musical instruments. Both you and your child can enjoy looking at, listening to, and making some noise while making the important choice of which instrument to play. Go to music stores, concerts, and even museums to explore this rich world of sound. For example, the Metropolitan Museum of Art in New York City has an entire hall devoted to musical instruments, and many natural history museums around the country feature instruments from various cultures and historical time periods.

This chapter covers the families of orchestral instruments and stand-alone instruments such as piano, guitar, and harp, listed in what's known as traditional score order: woodwinds, brass, strings, percussion, piano, and other instruments. The details included—appropriate ages to begin studying and relevant information about the instruments' physical attributes—should help steer you and your child to a good match.

Woodwinds

Woodwinds have existed in virtually all primitive cultures of the world. What could be simpler than blowing through a hollowed-out reed or animal bone or horn with holes in it to make different notes? In fact, some of the earliest undisputedly musical artifacts are thirty-two-thousand-year-old flutes made of bird bones that were found by archaeologists in caves in Germany and France. Our ancestors used them to communicate with each other, to call to animals, for ceremonial and religious purposes, and for self-entertainment. Early wind instruments evolved into pennywhistles, panpipes, and recorders, all held vertically while played, as are their descendants, including clarinet, oboe, and bassoon. By 1780, the clarinet could be found in most large European orchestras, and Mozart was the first composer to really exploit its potential. The orchestral flute developed around the same time, when it was found that a more powerful tone could be obtained blowing across the mouthpiece horizontally.

Woodwinds add color to the sound of large orchestras, wind ensembles, and chamber groups, and they are also featured instruments in orchestral and jazz settings. As students gain more experience playing their woodwind instrument, they will encounter a great variety of playing opportunities.

Recorders

Children who enjoy singing will enjoy the recorder. Recorders have been a first instrument for countless children. They are pleasurable to play, and a young player can easily achieve a pleasing sound. Recorders offer a way to learn the kind of controlled breathing that one needs for more advanced woodwind or brass instruments, without requiring a lot of lung power or stamina. They are also the least expensive authentic instrument you can buy.

Recorders range in size from the soprano (the size and pitch most commonly used in schools and as a starting instrument) to bass. The recorder is mechanically very simple. The player learns to find the right pitch; there are no valves or key pads, the child has to adjust his fingers to cover the holes and use just enough breath to get the right pitch. It is an ideal instrument for group lessons and is often taught in school music programs.

The advantages? Recorder is usually taught in small classes, and young children quickly learn how to blend their sound with others and what it feels like to make music with other children. The ease of learning simple tunes like "Hot Cross Buns" is empowering for beginners. Unfortunately, the instrument is treated mostly as a starter instrument, and children are not presented with more challenging material as time goes on; in fact, most professional players research their own repertoire using early music sources and advance on their own.

♪ *Age*: 5–7 (mostly); ideal for 6–9-year-olds

♪ *Repertoire*: Folk music, early music, and baroque

♪ *Cost*: $10 for a basic soprano; high quality or rare recorders can cost $100+

Flute

The modern metal flute is a melodic instrument with a beautiful sound, valued both as a solo instrument and for color and soaring above the ensemble in the orchestra. The sound is produced by blowing a controlled stream of air across the mouthpiece, not down through it (as one does for the other woodwinds). If your child can blow across the top of a bottle and get a sound, that's the idea. The flute has three sections that fit together, and it is held horizontally to the right side of the body. It's small, lightweight, and portable. Most beginners can play simple tunes by ear or with the help of written music after only a few weeks of practice, making it a popular choice. Fingering the notes is similar to the fingering on a recorder, which gives recorder players a head start. Beginning flute music is generally easy to read, which is also a plus.

Children are physically ready to play the flute when they can stand upright with a straight neck and hold the flute horizontally, with the left arm comfortable against the chest. Eight or nine is a good age to begin. Flutes with curved head joints are also available now, and they are easier for small children to play. But if your child noticeably twists his head and neck in the effort to play, he is physically too small to start playing the instrument. Because the player cannot see his fingers while playing, a student needs good coordination and control, much of which can be developed through study and practice.

The piccolo is not just a small flute, but a different instrument altogether. The mouthpiece is smaller than that of the flute, so it is more difficult to control the amount of air flowing into the instrument; it also requires greater dexterity since the key pads are smaller. It is better suited for intermediate and advanced flutists.

♪ *Age*: 8–9-year-olds; the flute is excellent for both pre-teens and teens; rapid progression can be made by older children

♪ *Cost*: Starting instrument $350; mid-priced $500–1500; professional quality $3,000+

Reeds

The largest subset of woodwinds is reed instruments. A thin reed clamped to a metal mouthpiece interrupts the airflow at the source, producing a strong, penetrating sound, somewhat like humming into a blade of grass. The player's breath makes the reed vibrate against the mouthpiece, then the vibration is amplified through the air column of the instrument. Clarinets and saxophones are single reed instruments. Oboes and bassoons (bassoons are the bass instrument of the woodwind family) are double reed instruments, which use two reeds bound together. They require tremendous breath control to play.

Clarinet. The clarinet, like the flute, is easy for beginners; one can produce a pleasing sound and play tunes within weeks. It is held vertically in front of the body, so the student can see her fingers. A child can learn to produce a big sound with little effort, as well as learn how to produce a range of sounds—sweet, piercing, woody, duck-like—depending in which octave she is playing. Clarinets have their own fingering system (fingers covering specific key pads to get different notes) and require coordination from both hands; a student can easily progress to saxophones, which have similar fingering and operate on the same principles. Students can make rapid progress and be able to play in a beginner's band or ensemble within a couple of months. The clarinet is a versatile instrument featured in orchestra, wind ensembles, and jazz repertoire.

♪ *Age*: 8+, when fingers can easily span the keys and cover the finger pads securely; great instrument for preteens and teens, easy transition to saxophone

♪ *Cost*: Starting instrument $250–350; mid-priced $400–800; professional quality $1,500–2,500

Saxophone. The saxophone, invented by Adolphe Sax in 1840, is the most modern instrument of the woodwinds. There are eight sizes of saxophones, but the most common are alto, tenor, and baritone. Saxophones are heavier than flute or clarinet so most children learn on alto, which weighs approximately five pounds, before progressing to the larger horns. The instrument requires strength and lung power. It is an easy transition from clarinet or flute (the fingering for alto is similar to flute), and sound production is similar to clarinet but the mouthpiece is much larger.

The saxophone is a good choice for students who like jazz and popular music. There are plenty of playing opportunities in concert bands, wind ensembles, marching bands, and even youth orchestras, in which parts are adapted for the instrument. The alto sax is a terrific starting instrument for teens; it is loud and noticeable, and a dedicated student can make rapid progress. The alto provides a good basis for learning to play all the saxophones, and possibly oboe and bassoon.

♪ *Age*: 11+; possible for younger students who have the physical strength and are very motivated; ideal for teens who have an affinity for jazz and pop.

♪ *Cost*: Starting alto instrument $600–750; mid-priced $1,200–1,500; professional quality $2,000+

Oboe. The oboe has a sweet sound, yet it can penetrate through the middle of a large orchestra (*Peter and the Wolf* is a good example). The oboe is usually picked up by older children who have started on recorder or clarinet and who fall in love with the instrument's uniqueness. Since the proper lip, tongue, and breathing techniques are tricky to acquire, the student needs to be determined and patient to deal with the oboe's technical challenges. The oboe is also a good instrument for tinkerers because oboe players usually cut and make their own reeds.

The oboe is related to a larger instrument called the English horn, which has a more mellow sound. Neither instrument is recommended for beginners. They are only rarely used in popular music or jazz settings, though there is a wealth of orchestral and wind ensemble music for both instruments.

♪ *Age*: 12+; possible for experienced younger students who are very motivated

♪ *Cost*: Starting instrument $500+; mid-priced $1,000–1,500; professional quality $3,500+

Bassoon. The bassoon is the largest woodwind, nearly five feet long, and has a warm woody sound that can express a range of moods. Like the oboe, many students come to the instrument because they fall in love with its sound and unique qualities. Having previous experience with other, simpler woodwinds is a plus. Students may also choose it as a second instrument because it will give them more playing opportunities (and more soloing opportunities) than being one among many flutists and clarinetists.

The bassoon is large, long, and heavy, so the best starting age is twelve or thirteen. Since, for the most part, it is a self-selecting instrument—students really come to it for its uniqueness—it can make an excellent first instrument for teens. One needs a wide hand and finger span and good coordination because the fingers and the keys are not visible while playing. The bassoon, like the oboe, has an unmistakable sound and is easily heard in orchestral solo passages, and even during ensemble passages. It is also often featured in music for wind ensembles and chamber groups.

♪ *Age*: 13+; experienced woodwind players who have the strength and coordination may start younger

♪ *Cost*: Starting instrument $2,000; mid-priced $3,000+; professional quality $5,000+

Brass

The brass family includes the loudest members of the orchestra, who can stand up to percussion at full blast. With their triumphant and majestic sound, these beautiful shiny instruments add color, drama, and power to the orchestra. During the Middle Ages, trumpets and sackbuts (early trombones) were traditionally used for fanfares, ceremonial music, and calls-to-arms. Brass instruments are still at the forefront of jazz and popular music; they are also the backbone of the orchestra and provide many opportunities to play in marching bands, jazz bands, and concert orchestras.

All brass instruments produce a big sound, and the stamina and exertion needed for sound production can provide a great release for very active children. The instruments range from small and light (the cornet) to big and cumbersome (the tuba), so they are suitable for a wide range of ages and sizes.

The sound is produced by controlled blowing (more like buzzing) through a cup-like mouthpiece. Tightening or relaxing the lips controls the pitch, as does the use of valves, keys, and the slide mechanism on the trombone. Each member of the brass family has its own shape mouthpiece and different size and length tubing, giving each its distinctive sound quality and range. Most brass instruments use only three fingers of the right hand for the valves, so unlike the woodwinds, dual-finger coordination is not required to produce noises of different pitches.

Trumpet. The trumpet is a flashy, extroverted instrument whose high register can soar above the orchestra or large jazz band. Physical size is not the criteria for your child to start trumpet as much as stamina, breath control, and strong teeth and gums. The trumpet and cornet are the smallest of the brass family and reach the highest notes. The hole in the cup-shaped mouthpiece is small, so it takes a lot of effort to force air through it for sound. Music for trumpet is usually very active. Trumpet parts will be busier and harder to read than those for the lower brass family, such as trombone and tuba. It is a good instrument for extroverts, but also for shy children who are daring and may need a new way to stand out. The trumpet requires a lot of patience and hard work to make real headway.

The cornet is a better starting instrument for seven- or eight-year-olds who have their hearts set on trumpet. One still needs strong teeth and gums, but it is lighter than a trumpet and is easier to produce a good sound. It is also a good preparatory instrument for any other members of the brass family.

♪ *Age*: 7–9 for cornet; 10+ for trumpet; possible for some motivated 9-year-olds
♪ *Cost*: Starting instrument $300–400; mid-priced $600–800; professional quality $1,000–2,000

French Horn. The French horn has a wholly different sound than the trumpet: velvety, echoing, and haunting. It is one of the most majestic members of the orchestra. Like the oboe and bassoon, students are drawn to it for its uniqueness and beautiful sound. It is a challenging instrument to play—even more so than the trumpet. Different pitches are produced by changing the size of the opening in the lips/mouth position (embouchure), and the student needs an excellent sense of pitch to play in tune. The left hand operates the three valves and the right hand is placed inside the bell of the horn, which helps to support the instrument. French horn players are always welcome in orchestras, chamber ensembles, and brass bands.

♪ *Age*: possibly as young as 9, especially if player transfers from another brass instrument.

♪ *Cost*: Starting instrument $850–1,000; mid-priced $1,500–1,800; professional quality $2,500–4,000

Trombone. The trombone is possibly the most versatile brass instrument of all. It is a very expressive instrument and can sound regal, lyrical, mellow, or witty, depending on the setting and style. The slide mechanism gives the instrument a human voice quality, and some jazz players indeed sound as if they are singing through the horn. Like the violin, the player has to form each note (in this case by adjusting the slide), which helps develop a good sense of pitch and intonation. Since the trombone has survived in roughly the same form since the Middle Ages, there is a wealth of music available, from early music to contemporary, including baroque, Renaissance, classical, pop, and jazz.

Though the trombone is long (when the slide is lengthened all the way it is five to six feet long), it is a not a heavy instrument to hold. The right arm needs to be long enough to control the slide comfortably. Like the other brass instruments, the student blows or buzzes into a cup-shaped mouthpiece, bigger than the mouthpiece on a trumpet. No valves or finger work are involved. Valve trombones do exist, but it is not generally considered an appropriate starting instrument. The trombone is elegant, at home in an orchestra, concert band, marching band, small jazz ensemble, or big band.

♪ *Age*: possibly as young as 9 or 10

♪ *Cost*: Starting instrument $350–450; mid-priced $600–800; professional quality $1,000–1,800

Tenor, Baritone, and Euphonium. The tenor and baritone horn are all small versions of the tuba and are good choices for beginning brass players, as well as good preparatory instruments for the more demanding members of the brass family. They are light and comfortable to play and require only a small amount of breath through large mouthpieces to produce the mellow, round sound that is characteristic of both horns. They are band instruments, not members of the orchestra, and most of the music written for them is fairly simple.

The euphonium, another cousin of the tuba, offers a good transition from the tenor and baritone horns. While the euphonium requires a little more strength and breath control, it is still easy to produce a good sound. It is an expressive and lyrical instrument with a rich mellow sound. It is at home in wind and brass ensembles and occasionally featured in orchestral music, but it is often a standout solo instrument in the world of brass band and wind ensembles. Many trombone players also play euphonium.

♪ *Age*: 9 or 10

♪ *Cost*: Starting instruments $1,200–1,500; mid-priced $2,500; professional quality $3,000+

Tuba. Believe it or not, the tuba, the biggest and lowest of the brass instruments, takes less energy to play than a piccolo or a trumpet. It is played like the rest of the brass family, by blowing or buzzing through the mouthpiece and changing lip and mouth position. It is the volume of the instrument, not the player, that acts as an amplifier and helps produce a big, deep sound that fills out the orchestral brass section, adding strength and heft.

The tuba is featured in brass ensembles and is used in the orchestra for large-scale works. It was an important instrument in early jazz, functioning as a bass. It has made a comeback in contemporary jazz ensembles of all sizes. Tuba players are always welcome in bands and orchestras, as it is not a commonly chosen instrument.

♪ Age: 12+

♪ Cost: Starting tuba $2,000–2,800; mid-priced $3,000–3,500; professional quality $4,000+

Strings

String instruments are simultaneously the most simply constructed instruments and among the most difficult to master. Like woodwinds, most string instruments have their roots in antiquity, but the refined violin and cello date back to the mid-1500s. The four major instruments—violin, viola, cello, and double bass—are all built the same way. They are essentially hollow boxes made of various sections of wood that are glued together (not nailed). Four strings are wrapped around pegs at the scroll of the instrument, attached to a tailpiece at the other end, and stretched across a bridge near the sound hole. The sound is produced when a bow is dragged across the strings or the strings are plucked, causing them to vibrate; the sound then resonates through the hollow box where it is amplified.

It sounds simple enough, but there are many challenges to learning this elegant and expressive family of instruments. There are no valves or frets to help your child find the right notes; the student needs to develop accurate pitch and learn the correct hand position to find them, as well as bowing technique. Strings require coordination, concentration, and the desire to make a beautiful sound.

The rewards for dedicated string students are many; achieving a unique personal sound and learning a rich and varied repertoire can be terrifically satisfying. Additionally, the strings offer a wide range of playing opportunities, in orchestral and chamber music settings, or for those who take on the added challenge to stand out as soloists. Players like Mark O'Connor and Allison Kraus, who have renewed the joy of fiddle music and jazz violin, can be very inspiring for children.

Violin

The violin has one of the most personally expressive sounds of all the instruments. It is the smallest and has the highest range of the string family. Violin students need a lot of supervision to get off to a good start, to develop a comfortable yet correct playing position from the very beginning. The violin is held under the chin; the left arm helps support the instrument while the left fingers work the fingerboard to get the correct pitch and the right hand does the bowing or plucking. The violin is also a physically expressive instrument—children can move with the music and develop an almost balletic posture. It is made in small sizes, ranging from 1/32 to 1/2 to full size, and can be started at a very young age. The sound is pleasing to young ears because the range falls within the range of children's voices. Playing the instrument is very much like singing—it is up to the child to make his own instrument sing. Students can play in ensembles from their earliest stages of learning, which can be very motivating.

- ♪ *Age*: 5+, but some Suzuki programs have children as young as 3
- ♪ *Cost*: Starting instrument $250; mid-priced $300–700; professional quality $1,500+

Viola

The viola is larger than the violin and has a mellower sound and a lower range. It is rarely chosen as a first instrument; children usually switch over from violin or another instrument at age twelve or thirteen. The switch is often suggested by a music teacher or orchestra director because there is always a need for viola players in school or youth orchestras. But many "switched-over" viola students fall in love with the instrument for its velvety sound and its less rigorous repertoire. The viola is not as widely available in small sizes as the violin is. Most students use full-size instruments, so be sure to take your child's size and arm length into consideration.

♪ *Age:* 12 (depending on child's size), if viola is first instrument

♪ *Cost:* Starting instrument $300; mid-priced $400–700; professional quality $1,500+

Cello

The cello is the easiest of the string family to play as a beginner and is available in small sizes. It is easier for beginners to achieve a good sound on it than on a violin for several reasons: it sits on its stem on the floor, supported by the player's legs; the fingerboard is wide and much easier for small fingers to find the right note position; the bow is bigger and easier to manipulate. The weight and left-hand stretch of full-size cellos make them suitable for children around twelve years of age and older. Though music for cello is written in the bass clef, beginning orchestra parts are fairly simple to read.

The cello is a beautifully expressive instrument, and children often respond to its dramatic sound. There is a vast repertoire for the instrument for solo, orchestra, and string quartet. Though starting cello may be easier than the other strings, real mastery takes years to achieve and requires conscientious study and practice.

♪ *Age*: 4+; most cellists begin as first instrument, though possible to use as second instrument

♪ *Cost*: Starting instrument $500–600; mid-priced $900–1,200; professional quality $1,500+

Double Bass

The double bass is the largest and lowest-sounding instrument of the orchestra, providing the bottom register and filling out a rhythmic function. Double basses are also made in small sizes, down to 1/10, but even so they stand taller than their player. The child must be strong enough to hold and control the instrument, which is played in a standing position (even if practiced sitting on a stool). Students often pick up the bass as a second instrument.

Bass players need to be facile at reading the bass clef, but most written bass music is not difficult to read because the instrument plays a supportive role in the orchestra. In jazz, however, the bass has long been a virtuoso instrument, especially in small ensembles where the instrument's depth and character is fully revealed.

♪ *Age*: 13+, often started as second instrument, or by students with an interest in jazz

♪ *Cost*: Starting instrument $1,000; mid-priced $1,500–2,000; professional quality $3,000+

Percussion

Percussion instruments also reach back to ancient times, when drumming was a means of secular communication as well as a call to the gods. Drumming, keeping up a steady rhythm, making sounds by tapping, pounding, and striking different objects is a natural inclination for children, and preschoolers are typically introduced to percussion instruments such as rattles, triangle, maracas, woodblocks, and more.

Most of us are familiar with the modern drum kit. This collection of instruments at the center of a rock 'n' roll band is played by one musician and includes a bass drum, a snare drum, several cymbals, and tom toms. The larger percussion family also includes pitched instruments such as xylophone, vibraphone, marimba, and tympani. A variety of percussion instruments are used in orchestral settings and in jazz, pop, and world music ensembles of every description.

For older children, studying percussion—in addition to drums—can be a comprehensive way to study music. Professional percussionists are well-versed musicians who read music notation and are required to study the pitched percussion instruments mentioned above. They are also skilled at playing an attractive battery of so-called percussive toys, including cymbals, gongs, triangles, woodblocks, and rain sticks.

Drums and percussion can be a great choice for active and even fidgety children. Drummers and percussionists are constantly moving from one object to another—changing sticks, mallets, and instruments—keeping the pulse and being aware of what everyone else is doing.

Drum kit

♪ *Age*: 8+, depending on coordination (usually start on snare drum alone); drum kit, 11+

♪ *Cost*: starting set $250–500; mid-priced $700–1,000; professional quality $2,000+

Xylophone, Vibraphone, Marimba, and Tympani

♪ *Age*: 12+, usually transfer from drums or keyboards

♪ *Cost*: Mallet instruments (vibraphone is most costly) starting $1,000–2,000; mid-priced $1,600–3,500; professional quality $2,500–5,000+

Tympani (pair) starting $3,500; mid-priced $4,200–4,500; professional quality $5,000+

Stand-Alone Instruments

Piano

The piano, with its scope, its many keys, and its versatility, power, and beauty, is captivating and magnetizing for many children. It is still one of the most popular starting instruments for many good reasons: it has a readily pleasing sound and children can quickly learn the logic of the instrument, and how to pick out tunes. The instrument's nature and construction also can provide a great opportunity to get a head start on learning about harmony and polyphony (playing more than one note at a time). But developing coordination and technique, learning to read two clefs simultaneously, and advancing on the instrument can be a frustrating process for many young children.

Though children can start as young as three or four (and many do), most children start between ages five and seven, even though this is still a challenging time in their lives because they are developing so many skills simultaneously. Successful piano study demands focused attention, patience, and good coordination. Children who enjoy working independently and who have fallen in love with the sound of the piano and its orchestral possibilities will happily spend hours at the instrument and will enjoy the challenge of reading and playing with both hands. There is a wealth of piano music for players at any level, from the beginner to the virtuoso.

Other keyboard-based instruments include historic instruments such as harpsichord, clavier, organ, as well as state-of-the-art electronic keyboards, synthesizers, and digital pianos. Most piano teachers prefer teaching on the acoustic instru-

ment, which has a far different touch and response than its digital counterpart, which produces sound electronically.

♪ *Age*: may start as early as 3 or 4, most children start around 5; often started as second instrument or by students with an interest in jazz or popular music

♪ *Cost*: Spinet: low price $2,000; mid-priced $3,000; high quality $3,500

Console or Studio: $2,500–3000; mid-priced $3,500+; high quality $5,000

Grand: $6,000; mid-priced $10,000+; high quality $15,000+

Guitar

The classical guitar is a descendant of the lute family. It has six nylon strings stretched over the sound hole and bridge to a wooden body, which resonates when the strings are plucked or strummed. Unlike the violin family, the neck of the guitar has frets to determine notes. It comes in small sizes—1/4, 1/2, and 3/4—and may be started by very young children. It is easy to learn how to play simple chords and accompany oneself or others singing, making it a perennially popular instrument. Just like any other instrument, true mastery requires patience, effort, and an affinity for the instrument. The guitar is ideal for children who love rock 'n' roll, blues, and pop music but can also apply themselves to learning the intricacies of the instrument. An ambitious and inspired student can head in the direction of rock virtuoso Jimi Hendrix, Brazilian guitar master Romero Lubambo, classical master Andrés Segovia, or contemporary flamenco artists the Gipsy Kings.

♪ *Age*: 5, or when children can hold instrument easily and when lefthand fingers can stretch

♪ *Cost*: starting instrument $150; mid-priced $250–400; high quality $1,000+

Harp

Just as the guitar has several variations (six-string, twelve-string, full-bellied) and is related to several other instruments (mandolin, ukulele), there are several kinds of harps. They range from the folk harp and small Irish harp to the large concert pedal harp. Today, it is common to hear the concert harp not only in orchestral settings but often as a solo instrument, in a chamber group, and even in some jazz ensembles.

While a child can start the Irish and folk harps at a young age, nine or ten is better for the concert harp because it requires far more strength than the delicacy of its sound implies. It takes a lot of coordination and technique to get good articulation from the strings and to manipulate the pedals. For instance, you have to bring your fingers all the way into the palm to get a good clean sound from the strings. A good position requires upper arm strength because the student needs to hold his or her arms parallel to the floor and hold the fingers in a certain shape while keeping the wrists loose. The pedal harp is a chromatic instrument; the pedals are used to adjust the pitch. Another option is the lever harp, which uses levers to set the specific key to be played.

Parents should be aware of the logistics and impracticalities of the harp. First of all, music stores do not carry harps, so if your child is interested in testing one, your first step is to locate a harpist who will help your child appreciate the scope of the instrument. Many professional harpists teach, and your child will most likely use the teacher's harp at a lesson. But, when it is necessary to transport the harp, a parent's help will of course be needed. Daily practicing can become problematic if your child only has the use of an instrument at a teacher's home or at school, but dedicated students and their families learn to work out these logistics, in much the same way that tympani players and students of other cumbersome instruments do.

♪ *Age*: folk harp at 8 or 9; concert harp, 9+

♪ *Cost*: Folk harp: starting instrument $750–1,500; mid-priced $2,000; high quality $4,500

 Pedal harp: $8,000; high quality $28,000+

Miscellaneous Instruments

Pennywhistles, kazoos, mellophones, and harmonicas are all good starting instruments for young children. They can be introduced in a simple way and are ideal for families to learn and play together. Exposure to masterful playing on such instruments or other folk instruments can lead your child into the world of music making or inspire an eventual desire to play a more complex instrument.

Good Sounds and Informative Instrument Web Sites

The Clarinet Pages—The Young People's Pages
www.woodwind.org/clarinet

International Clarinet Home Page
www.clarinet.org

International Double Reed Society
http://idrs.colorado.edu/

International Horn Society
www.hornsociety.org

Jazz for Young People
www.jalc.org/educ/curriculum
Online jazz curriculum for introducing children to jazz instruments, historic figures, development of the music, and more.

The New York Philharmonic Kidzone
www.nyphilkids.org
Children's site for The New York Philharmonic includes playful and informative presentations of instruments, conductors, composers, games, and more.

SFS Kids—The San Francisco Symphony
www.sfskids.org
An excellent, informative, and entertaining children's Web site for the San Francisco Symphony.

The Trombone Page
www.missouri.edu/~cceric/

Finding a Teacher

"I can't stress enough how important finding the right teacher is."
—Paula Robison, flutist

"The child really needs to love the teacher."
—Eve Weiss, guitar teacher

"The child's door to the musical world is the teacher."
—Jonathan Partridge, trumpet instructor

September. It's back-to-school time. You and your child have already decided on an instrument to start studying this fall. This, plus soccer on Tuesday and swim team on Thursday, fills your week.

But planning for music lessons takes more time than signing up for soccer or swim team, and finding the right music teacher is an important part of the back-to-school crunch. You may get lucky through a great match that comes from word-of-mouth or having an excellent community music school nearby. Otherwise, the process of finding the right teacher takes research—as much as finding the right preschool or pediatrician. This relationship, especially if it's your child's first music teacher, is the key to your child's musical education.

This chapter explores issues regarding clarifying musical goals for your child and outlines a range of questions to ask prospective music teachers. These suggestions should help you narrow your search for the right teacher for your child. What you don't want to narrow, though, is the sense of possibility that a good teacher can inspire.

Finding the Right First Teacher

Are you one of the legions of adults who hated piano lessons and quit? Or did you stop playing in the school band because it wasn't fun? What happened (other than becoming a teenager)? Many of us quit because of unsympathetic teachers. These can come in several guises. There were those who didn't give us *any* music we liked working on; others were too formulaic or rigid in their approach.

As you start seeking a good match for your child, try to envision what will or won't create a good learning relationship. Beware the teacher who is too strict (in the guise of "music as discipline"), doesn't really enjoy working with children, or is too demanding for your child's temperament. Also watch out for a mediocre, poorly trained teacher who may handicap a beginning student by incorrectly advising him on technique.

What are the key things to look for in a teacher? Certainly, experience, the ability to convey the joy of making music, a willingness to impart both good technique and musical sensitivity, and a plan for introducing a properly sequential and appealing repertoire. But perhaps the most important thing is to find someone who really likes working with children and can establish a good rapport with his students. In one study, the British psychologist Dr. John Sloboda found that a majority of high-achieving music students remembered the personal warmth of their early teachers rather than their musical expertise. In many instances the teacher was the nice old lady down the road who loved music, loved children, and could communicate both.

Every child is different, so think about what teaching style may best fit your child. That first teacher has to be able to get your child excited about what it means to work on music—to concentrate, to experiment, to discover the power of sound, and to tell stories through sound. Some methods and approaches, such as Dalcroze and Orff Schulwerk, train their teachers to bring out the playfulness of young students and tap into their exploratory nature. In a private setting, some children thrive with a demanding, professional conservatory-style teacher whose methods are highly structured and who expects a lot of practice time; others need a far more gentle, playful, and flexible approach. Some children may do better with one-on-one instruction; for others the social nature of a small group will be more inspiring, as well as more fun (and less expensive). Also think about what environment might be best, a music school or studio where your child can be around his or her peers, or at home.

Musical Goals

First, give some thought to your musical goals for your child, in addition to inspiring a genuine love of music. For example, your goal might be for your child to gain the self-discipline that comes with regular practicing and incremental achievement. Larry Malin, a trumpet teacher and band instructor, says that one thing that keeps him teaching is seeing "the intrinsic reward a child gets from not being able to do something and then working on it and getting it—from being able to do a skill one day that they couldn't do yesterday."

Other extramusical benefits include a better attention span, sharper focus, and increased memory retention—in other words, they are all life skills that will be valuable to your child every day. These benefits are currently the subjects of numerous studies being conducted by neuroscientists and psychologists who are researching the ways instrumental study affects children's learning abilities. "I preach this all the time—studying music carries over to other areas of learning, like reading," Malin says. "It's not an accident. The school with the highest reading level in New York City is the Special Music School. Kids who focus on music focus more efficiently in other areas, too." (See chapter 9 for more information on the subject.)

Give some thought to the range of musical options you want to present to your child. Do you want a teacher who will focus only on classical music or someone who can present other styles (jazz, pop, country, folk) that your child might have more of an affinity for? Do you want the teacher to pay attention to particular skills such as sight-reading and improvisation? Brenda Dillon, program director of the National Piano Foundation and a lifelong piano educator, believes in giving young students, even at the simplest level, the skills that go beyond the basics of the instrument. "What do we give people for life when we give our children music lessons? The adults who are still playing the piano long after childhood lessons, are the people who I call functional musicians. They know how to sight-read, how to improvise, transpose—

they really were taught how to be functional musicians." A teacher who can impart age- and skill-appropriate doses of music theory and history into the lesson can genuinely inspire your child.

Finally, you need to make sure the lessons work within your family budget and schedule without strain. The daily demands of school, other activities, homework, and your own work are all factors that need to be seriously considered.

Once you've clarified at least some of your goals, here are some ways to help you proceed in your search for the ideal music teacher for your child.

- ♪ Get recommendations. Ask friends, teachers, public or private school music teachers, after-school program coordinators, and others in your community for teacher referrals. Word-of-mouth can lead you to excellent teachers, but it's still worth your time to get several references. After all, a teacher who is great for your best friend's child may not be so great for yours.

- ♪ Check with local schools. Community music schools, conservatories, or music programs at colleges and universities may have excellent teachers on staff or have referral lists available for families.

- ♪ Research the educational programs that may be available through regional symphonies, chamber groups, jazz organizations, and youth orchestras. They can often also refer teachers.

- ♪ Check out professional organizations, including your local chapter of a national organization such as the National Association for Music Education (MENC), the American String Teachers Association (ASTA), and the American Music Conference (AMC). These regional offices should be able to provide referrals.

- ♪ Ask a local music store if it has a referral lists or even an on-site teacher.

♪ Check the yellow pages and other directory resources. The local yellow pages, classified advertisements, and the Internet can be good starting places, but be especially thorough about checking the teacher's credentials and asking for several references.

Once you have narrowed down the recommendations to three or four choices, you are ready to consider each candidate more carefully.

Interviewing Teachers

When you finally have your first conversation with a prospective teacher, be prepared with specific questions, particularly about the teacher's qualifications, experience with children, and overall approach. Faculty credentials are usually readily available at music schools, university-affiliated programs, or music studios. However there are some things you need to find out for yourself, by conversing with the teacher directly or through the program or school director. A busy, well-qualified teacher will have questions for you, too—about your child's musical experience and interest, your musical goals, how much time your child may be able to practice, and how much time you will be able to devote to your child's musical education. The two of you can then quickly decide whether it's worthwhile to have a first meeting or not.

This is the information you need to gather from a prospective teacher:

♪ The teacher's qualifications, including the number of years she has spent teaching, whether she has a degree in music or any other special certification

♪ How much experience she has with young children and beginners

♪ How many students does the teacher already have? If a teacher has more than thirty-five students, that is a full load. You should be wary of the teacher being over-committed.

♪ The prospective teacher's specializations: age groups, playing ability, style, practice expectations, sensitivity to your child's age and musical experience

♪ Performance opportunities: how many recitals or concerts a year will your child participate in?

♪ Musical styles: does she concentrate solely on classical music or does she introduce other styles in the course of lessons?

♪ Teaching materials: what particular method books, instructional software, videos, or electronic equipment will be used?

♪ Basic fees per lesson time (thirty minutes, forty-five minutes, or an hour) and policies regarding fees and cancellations

There is other information you might want to know about a teacher's working methods. Does the teacher give guidance to parents about how the student should practice at home? How does the teacher set goals for his students and assess progress? Some music schools or studios give out periodic progress reports, and some teachers are happy to discuss progress and problems at length on the phone (apart from the student's lesson time), whereas others won't. It's good to know what a teacher's protocol or a school's policy is regarding communication with parents.

There are several ways you can further check out prospective teachers before committing your child to lessons. You can ask if it's possible to attend a recital of the teacher's students, or even a performance by the teacher herself. Community music

schools typically hold open houses, featuring student performances, in the fall with their teachers on hand for discussion.
Many teachers and music programs offer a trial lesson, often
at a reduced rate or no charge at all (always inquire).

Trial lessons reveal quite a bit: right away, you can see
how the teacher relates to your child. You can observe his
manner (strict or casual, warm or a little reserved) and how
he introduces himself and the instrument. If you found a
teacher through word of mouth, bear in mind that someone
else's child will have a different kind of teacher-student relationship and different needs than yours might. One friend
says that she really appreciates her son's teacher because he
keeps her easily distracted son focused—that is more important for her than where the teacher got his degree or where
he performed last.

Sometimes, changes of circumstance can have unexpected positive effects. For instance, last year my son's private
teacher moved. I had to find a new violin teacher, and we
enrolled him at a community music school not too far away.
In one fell swoop, everything seemed to change for the better. Alex was now in a bustling musical environment with
plenty of friendly kids running in and out for lessons. Also,
he signed up with a male teacher, which proved a beneficial
choice for my ten-year-old boy. Chris, the new teacher, was
young and cool but had already been teaching classical violin for several years. He also taught fiddle music and early
jazz styles, which Alex had been exploring and really liked.
Practicing became a lot less "nudgy." That's a relief for any
parent. The school also offered a wider range of performance opportunities. There were frequent informal recitals
that motivated students at all levels to polish up their work
and gain self-confidence.

It Takes All Kinds

Some people think they are good enough to teach, but really have insufficient training and just want to make a little extra money. When our neighbor's fourteen-year-old son wanted to learn guitar, he took lessons from an eighteen-year-old college student who posted a flyer at the local library. The girl proved a terrible teacher, and the student, intimidated by her bossy and untrained teaching style, has not picked up the guitar since.

Even among classical teachers in acclaimed programs, there can be worrisome incidents. Elizabeth, now thirteen, has been studying violin at a prestigious preparatory program since she was seven. Her private teacher encouraged her to apply for the program, and she continued studying with him there once she was accepted. But after a few months, she was crying every day. Her teacher had become harsh with her. "Their relationship was just falling apart," said her mother. "He would scream at her, 'Why don't you play with a straight bow?' And she would come out crying. I asked her if she wanted to quit violin, and she said, 'No, I just want to change teachers.'"

Her family had no experience with music, let alone the rarified world of conservatories with prestigious teachers and prep programs. Elizabeth's mother called the director and was able to schedule trial lessons with a couple of other teachers. One of them was young and inexperienced but clicked immediately with Elizabeth. "My new teacher was young," Elizabeth recalled. "My (former) teacher was very upset because he felt the new one was a novice—and he was a great god or whatever. But he didn't have to be anyone famous for us—we picked him out of instinct. I really liked him—he was nice, and I understood what he meant, he explained things well.

And, he was just friendly. My parents liked him." Seven years later, Elizabeth is still studying with him.

How much do credentials and degrees matter? That depends on you and the musical goals you have for your child. Private music teachers are not legally required to have any kind of certification or degree—that goes for the guitar teacher in the music store or the most experienced children's piano teacher in the neighborhood.

Currently, there is a growing trend for music teachers to become certified, and certain methods, such as Suzuki, Orff Schulwerk, and Kodály, confer certification on teachers who meet their own training requirements. Many music teachers belong to professional organizations such as the National Association for Music Education (MENC), and their regional offices may be able to provide referrals (see the end of this chapter for contact information). While on-staff music teachers at public schools must be certified classroom teachers, the credentials for part-time music teachers vary widely and are up to the discretion of the school.

To me, however, it is far more reassuring if Dr. Sloboda's "nice old lady down the street" has a music degree, which—hopefully—would indicate that she has comprehensive musical training and thus can offer more sensitive musicianship and methodical instruction to your child.

What to beware of? Celebrity teachers who may be overbooked, people who claim you can "play guitar in ten easy lessons," and teachers who are very quick to tell you that your child is gifted.

Here are a list of key terms to be aware of when researching a music teacher's qualifications:

♪ Music degree: A Bachelor of Music degree would mean the graduate has completed a comprehensive course in theory, history, and performance on his or her instrument.

♪ Specializations: Music majors and graduate students may also specialize in any number of additional areas, such as music education, conducting, composition, or jazz studies.

♪ Pedagogy: In response to a growing interest, an increasing number of conservatories and music departments are offering courses in pedagogy (the art of teaching). This can help accomplished young performers become better equipped to teach.

♪ Student teachers: They may have teaching positions in a conservatory under the supervision of master teachers.

♪ Professional musicians as teachers: Many active professional musicians also teach, some with more training in professional teaching than others.

When you have chosen a music teacher, it is completely appropriate to ask her if you can sit quietly at the first few lessons to observe her style and, more significantly, the way she and your child relate to each other. Is your child attentive, engaged, and cooperative? Is his or her interest sparked? Does he or she ask questions that reveal curiosity and a desire to know more? Does your child walk out of the lesson excited? This is an important relationship you're creating, and, since you have more choice in the matter than you do in the choice of your child's schoolteacher, go for the sparkle! Even more, says Eve Weiss: "The student has to really love the teacher—that's the only way it can work."

Musical Chairs

Finding the right match in a teacher will help lay the groundwork for success, which means helping create a positive routine for lessons and practicing and making music an active part of your family life. A large part of your search for a teacher should include figuring out the right setting for the lessons—home, studio, or music school. How busy is your household? Do you want someone to come to your house, or can you take your child to lessons? You will find a wider range of first-rate instructional venues than in decades past.

Here are some of the options available to you:

♪ Private lessons at your home. There are many excellent music teachers who still make house calls, especially young teachers just starting to develop their clientele. Some children do better in familiar surroundings, and it may give parents more opportunities to observe the lessons or at least remain within earshot. However, a teacher might charge more because of commuting time and related expenses.

♪ Private lessons in the teacher's home or studio.

♪ Community music schools are certified by the National Guild of Community Schools of the Arts. Your child will have access to small group instrumental classes, chamber groups, and theory classes. There are frequent student and faculty recitals, both formal and informal. Community music schools traditionally accept students of all ages and levels and offer a friendly, supportive musical community. Faculty members generally have music degrees.

♪ Cooperative studios, such as the Drummer's Collective in New York City, are typically formed by a group of teachers who share rental space, equipment, and expertise. Such cooperatives may offer group lessons and specialized classes or instruction.

♪ Music stores may have on-site lessons on a variety of instruments; however, the standard of teaching may not be as good as at community music schools, which have an educational mission.

♪ Conservatory preparatory programs including Juilliard and the Manhattan School of Music in New York City, the Curtis Institute in Philadelphia, and the New England Conservatory in Boston offer preparatory programs to intermediate and advanced students between five and eighteen years old who must audition for acceptance. Private instruction and ensembles are taught by master teachers and distinguished artists. These programs offer intensive training for serious students, and there are high expectations for commitment and practicing. Prep programs can be very expensive, but deserving students are encouraged to apply for scholarships.

♪ College or university preparatory programs. Regional colleges and universities that have strong music departments often have their own preparatory programs (similar to conservatory prep programs that require auditions) or programs that serve the larger community. They offer lessons and classes for all levels, which may be taught by student teachers under supervision, with fees varying accordingly.

♪ Community programs run under the umbrella of regional orchestras or other arts organizations. For example, the Armstrong Community Music School, the community arm of the Austin Lyric Opera Company, is one of the first community music schools in Texas. It offers instruction in classical, jazz, and a variety of other musical styles, while also providing specific opera outreach programs for schools.

Community music schools have become increasingly popular and valuable resources, with excellent faculty and an interesting range of programs. For example, the Eastman Community Music School is under the auspices of the acclaimed Eastman School of Music in Rochester, New York. Some faculty members are on the Eastman College faculty, and others are active performers and educators at other schools in the area. They are all committed to the highest level of excellence in teaching. The Community Music School of Springfield, Massachusetts, has affordable and high-quality programs for all ages and runs innovative music programs for high-risk teens in their own neighborhoods.

For many young children the solo nature of studying and practicing an instrument such as the piano can become too isolating an experience. Finding an appropriate, complementary class at a music school or switching from private lessons at home to a community music school or arts program may rescue a child who is ready to give up on lessons. Switching gears to keep your child happily involved in music is fine. It may take a couple of attempts to find the appropriate venue, as your child's musical needs and interests develop.

Lesson Fees. Fees for lessons vary considerably in different parts of the country. For instance, in New York City, Boston, San Francisco, and other metropolitan areas, the average fee is thirty dollars for a thirty-minute private lesson and forty-five dollars for forty-five minutes; fees for renowned teachers can run as much as eighty dollars an hour and far more. By contrast, in smaller cities and regions throughout the country, private lessons average fifteen to twenty dollars for a thirty-minute lesson; thirty dollars for forty-five minutes.

Community music schools follow a similar trend. At the Community Music School of Springfield in western Massachusetts, about ninety miles outside of Boston, fees for private lessons for a seventeen-week semester are twenty-three dollars for a thirty-minute lesson, and thirty-five dollars for forty-five minutes. These are approximately the same rates as the Eastman Community School. For an eighteen-week semester at Armstrong Community Music School (formed by the Austin Lyric Opera) in Austin, Texas, private lessons run twenty dollars for thirty minutes, thirty dollars for forty-five minutes; small group keyboard classes or Suzuki classes cost $225. Some schools offer reduced rates for so-called buddy lessons. These are attractive, reasonable rates for programs that have reputable faculties and a variety of classes.

Conservatory preparatory programs are the most costly. Typically, their programs include private lessons, a theory class, an appropriate ensemble, and extra technique classes. The fee for the prep program at Mannes College of Music in Manhattan is eighteen hundred dollars a semester; for Manhattan School of Music it can range from $2,230–2,630, depending on the length of the private lesson. There are usually surcharges for select private teachers from the college faculty, too.

Most music schools and prep programs offer scholarships for deserving students or sliding scale fees; community music schools try not to turn anyone away for financial reasons. Some private teachers are also willing to offer a sliding scale fee for promising students.

These days there are also a greater variety of outreach programs; some operate through the public schools, while others are run by conservatories, community music schools, symphonies, chamber groups, and youth orchestras. For example, the InterSchool Orchestras (ISO) of New York offers free private lessons to deserving students already in the orchestra. Its Teaching Intern Program (TIP), also noteworthy, pairs ISO high school orchestra members with students who want to start learning an instrument. Juilliard sponsors in-school partnerships with several underserved New York City elementary schools for low-cost or free private and small-group lessons, with Juilliard student teachers acting as instructors. The New England Conservatory in Boston has a similar program. Check your local conservatory to see if it provides anything along the same line.

Lesson Duration. A thirty-minute lesson is just the right amount of time for beginners and very young children. For more experienced children, a forty-five-minute lesson is desirable, as there will be more material for your child to cover in any given lesson. Bear in mind, music teachers are generally a very dedicated group of professionals. Most are generous with their time, when they're not pressed by another student at the door. My son's forty-five-minute lesson often stretches to an hour, and he is not aware of how much time goes by!

Other Expenses. The extra expenses for music lessons are not too daunting, with the exception of electronic instruments (the sky's the limit for synthesizers, keyboards, amplifies, and software). Your child's teacher will be able to advise you on these incidentals, but, as a general guide, you should be prepared to allow approximately thirty dollars for methods books and whatever you can reasonably afford beyond that for CDs, tapes, or concert tickets to inspire you child. Use your local resources: many local public libraries have sheet music and classical CDs and DVDs available.

Learning Styles and Teaching Styles

In some cases, the teacher is the child's only live musical model and needs to be a first-rate multitasker. The lesson should be peppered with brief examples played by the teacher, so your child can closely observe the beautiful sound, good posture, and correct positioning.

Once your child has been studying for a year or two, an introduction to music theory (through the lens of her particular instrument) can further her understanding of Western musical heritage—musical forms, kinds of compositions, different styles and periods of music, what scales are, and more. A good private teacher can impart this during private lessons and can suggest other supplementary resources, theory books, or even a special theory class. A versatile teacher can also enrich your child's musical education by encouraging an interest in composers and their lives and by giving the music some historical context (for example, explaining that minuets were dances).

But the most critical ingredient is still the teacher's relationship with your child. A sensitive teacher can quickly ascertain how a particular child learns, whether he is perfectionist, impulsive, methodical, competitive, and so forth and will work within those limitations, instead of trying to fit your child into a strict schedule of accomplishment. If a child walks into a lesson complaining of being tired, the teacher might need to "trick" him by saying it will be a short lesson or by suggesting they work on the child's favorite material first. Skilled teachers can turn wily children around and distract them into a productive session. Energy, enthusiasm, patience, firmness, flexibility, and psychological insight all factor in. The master pianist and teacher Menahem Pressler described his approach as "a constantly shifting mix of firmness, kindness, and humor cannily geared to the needs of each individual."

Teacher's POV. If your child has reached a plateau with his or her music lessons or is starting to complain about them vehemently, it can be useful to think about the process from the teacher's point of view. Some teachers have high musical expectations and want to work with children who will rise to them. Other teachers have a more relaxed attitude about what skills they expect students to develop and about practicing expectations.

Are there teachers who can work with students who are clearly taking lessons at their parents' insistence and refuse to practice at all? Yes. Many experienced, creative, and patient teachers do just that, often by necessity, and eventually win their students over with goodwill and a flexible approach. Such teachers want kids to have fun with music, get some basic musicianship, and become exposed to what it means to study an instrument. Both kinds of teachers—and all the gradations in between—have their place in the world of music education.

Teaching Your Own Children. In truth, we as parents are our children's first music teachers. We are the ones who have first sung to them, hummed to them, danced with them, and clapped with them. Those of us who have studied an instrument also have the option of teaching our own children—if we have the instrument, an extraordinary amount of patience, and a methodical way of going about it.

Anecdotally, many parents with musical training start out by teaching their own children. Many parents will give their students rudimentary skills on an instrument to get them going; others manage to be teacher and parent simultaneously.

William Starr, a violin teacher and author of *To Learn with Love* (an instructional, inspirational, and witty guide about music, children, and parenting), and his wife taught music to all eight of their children. Starr's youngest son would even stand on the toilet seat in the morning while his father was shaving to practice because that was the only time he and his father could be alone together. The Starrs' case is pretty extreme—most of us can barely get one child to practice without causing a huge uproar.

"No, I think it's insanity," says Eve, a guitar teacher who, while not officially her son's violin teacher, is very involved with her eleven-year-old son's daily practice sessions. "I think you need a bad guy. The teacher has to be the one who says, 'I want you to do it *this* way!' Then you can just back it up at home. But the point is you *need* to back it up. There are very few children who know how to practice what the teacher wants on their own."

Sam Amidon is an accomplished fiddler with an up-and-coming music career. His parents are both music educators in Vermont who give teacher-training seminars to elementary school teachers around the country. Sam's father, Peter, was his teacher for three years—until it was time for him to "learn to read music. Then I turned him over to someone else," said Peter. "It was too frustrating for both of us."

But Peter Amidon gave his son far more than his first music lessons. The community in which they live in Vermont has a vibrant music culture—unusual for a small town today. "There was a big value placed on music in the community," said Peter. "Sam grew up hearing people singing in our living room and playing all kinds of instruments, many different styles. Everyone he knew played music."

As in all family pursuits, you need to feel your way through what is possible with your children. If you are adept at an instrument and have the patience and playfulness to teach your children *and* make sure they practice, go for it. But as your child progresses, you may find that just keeping up a good practicing routine is a way of teaching your child, and maintaining it certainly requires a lot of tact and finesse. One of Sloboda's surveys of conservatory students showed that all of them "had parents who took an active participatory role in music lessons and daily practice. All these students' parents supervised their children's early practice on a moment-to-moment basis."

The students indicated that had their parent not pushed them to practice, they probably wouldn't have done so much practicing. Flute virtuoso Paula Robison said that when she was a young teenager and told her father that she wanted to be a musician, he said to her, "OK, but I'm going to make you practice—that's the only way it will happen."

Resources

American String Teachers Association (ASTA)
1806 Robert Fulton Drive
Reston, VA 22091
(703) 476-1316
www.astaweb.com
State and regional branches give referrals for private teachers. This organization also sponsors string programs in certain communities and schools. ASTA also holds conferences, teacher workshops, and competitions for students.

Music Teachers National Association (MTNA)
The Varew Tower
441 Vine Street, Suite 505
Cincinnati, OH 45202
(513) 421-1420
www.mtna.org
MTNA is a supporting organization for school-affiliated music teachers at all levels, from elementary through university. Promotes highest standards for performance and teaching for all instruments. Provides contacts for regional offices and teacher referrals.

National Association for Music Education (MENC)
1806 Robert Fulton Drive
Reston, VA 22091
(800) 336-3768
www.menc.org
This is a valuable site regarding school music programs; also links to regional offices and resources.

National Guild of Community Schools of the Arts (NGCSA)
P.O. Box 8018
Englewood, NJ 07631
(201) 871-3337
www.nationalguild.org
The National Guild offers membership to schools based on quality of faculty, curriculum, facilities, community outreach, and more.

National Piano Foundation
4021 McEwen Street
Dallas, TX 75244
(214) 233 9107
www.pianonet.com
This Web site provides links to regional offices and teacher listings.

Practice, Practice, Practice

"If you don't practice now, I'll take away your allowance!"

"If you don't practice now, you can't watch TV!"

"If you don't practice now, forget about that new computer game!"

Or a bigger allowance. Or going to the movies this weekend. Or using instant messenger. Or . . . or . . .

Sound familiar? Practicing remains one of the biggest hurdles to studying an instrument happily and successfully—and one of the biggest sore points between parents and children. Yet there is no more fundamental key to success on an instrument and to the kind of musical accomplishment and satisfaction that helps children become self-motivated about music. Learning what to practice, how to practice, how much to practice, and what constitutes a productive practice session turns the tide from lackluster playing to playing with technical ease and musical expression. Practicing can also turn a slowly progressing child's frustration and discouragement into the excitement that comes with tangible achievement: "Look, Mom—I played the whole thing!"

So why is practicing still such a struggle? What is it about practicing that turns a child's happy musical interest into a power play, and how can we avoid that? To answer this, we first have to back up a moment. Why do we practice at all? What does practicing an instrument really mean?

What Practicing Means

Practicing is very different than playing an instrument for fun, exploring an instrument, or pecking out tunes by ear—all things most children engage in quite happily and naturally. In fact, practicing—playing a song or a pattern in a particular way and repeating it to perfection—goes against almost any child's inclination to explore spontaneously and freely. Kids might find the word "training," as in baseball training, much easier to take. In truth, there are many similarities between practicing music and honing an athletic skill. Both involve a regular time investment and a lot of repetition—all to make the uncomfortable comfortable and to turn something hard into something easy and fluid. Practicing is buzzing through a mouthpiece for five minutes straight or playing long steady notes on a trombone. Practicing is playing the same tricky section of a piece of music several times every day until it flows out almost unconsciously through the fingertips. Practicing is playing scales or études but trying to make them sound beautiful. Practicing is also learning to read music, holding the violin and bow correctly for twenty whole minutes, or sitting at the piano without slumping. The goal of practicing is to give the student the physical, intellectual, and even the expressive skills to make the music come alive.

Regardless of a student's age or musical experience, effective instrumental practice is completely goal-oriented and can be technical and creative at the same time. Your child's teacher should have a curriculum and repertoire that can be tailored to help your child to build consistency in sound production, physical ease, and musical understanding. To achieve these goals, practicing means concentrating, focusing on the small things that add up to big things, and learning to express oneself through sound.

There is no getting around the fact that practicing is hard work, even when our children reveal a deep love for and interest in music and instruments. It is a far more demanding activity than the other chores about which we insist "you have to" and nudge our children to complete. It is not the same as asking them to clean their room or take swim lessons or go to soccer practice. It can often demand more concentration and intellectual effort than regular homework. So it's best if you can make practicing as routine and predictable as mealtimes or brushing teeth. And provide yourself with tools and tricks to deflect fights with your child and help him or her deal with the frustrating moments that will inevitably arise.

Eve Weiss witnesses and participates in practicing struggles from the dual vantage points of an experienced guitar teacher and a parent of a budding musician. She and her son have certainly had flare-ups about practicing, but the family has also had a system in place since her son began lessons at the age of three. The routine they began at that time was five minutes in the morning and five minutes at night. Now it's an hour before school and another after dinner. The way her son organizes his sessions is his own decision. Sometimes he works on his classical material in the morning, sometimes he works on his jazz repertoire. His experience with practicing has not been without stress, strain, and fights, but it has undoubtedly helped him become an accomplished young musician. These days, he's pretty cooperative about putting in his two hours a day on the violin since he performs professionally several times a year. He enjoys the challenge of mastering tricky musical passages and working out improvisational ideas, but there is no question that the routine of practicing became part of his life years ago. "You have to set up a system," said his mother.

> The important thing is the routine, the routine, the routine—and not to be scared to tell your child "You have to do this." I understand that fear—you're scared to squash your kid's love of music or an instrument. On the other hand, if you really make them take lessons and study an instrument, they'll love it more because they can do it! And if they don't want to do it, no amount of you making them do it is going to make them want to do it.
>
> Kids need a routine, and they need boundaries. Jonathan's friend Peter is a student of mine, and his mother told me, "Well, if my kid was as talented as Jonathan I would make him practice two hours a day, too."
>
> But that's not the point—you've got to get kids practicing early on so it becomes part of their life. When we were pushing Jonathan to practice at three years old we had no idea what he was. What we did know was that he loved music—and most kids do love music. Some parents say, "Oh, I'll let my kids practice when they want to, I won't force them because they should be free," but that just doesn't work. Kids need the security of knowing Mommy and Daddy are going to tell them what to do and when to do it. Then within that, you let them choose—the order of the pieces, or how many repetitions. Or you could say, "OK, you get to pick the

practice time, but this is going to be your practice time every single day."

Practicing involves different kinds of physical and intellectual problem solving. Physically, the problems include standing or sitting with the correct posture and hand position, learning good intonation, and learning how to sustain a long note. Intellectual problems range from analyzing a new rhythm to grasping the form of a piece. No matter how old your child is, the acknowledgment that you've been listening and rewarding them with praise or a favorite snack when a problem has been solved or a challenge has been met can help sustain your child's goodwill about practicing.

Different Ages and Stages

Practicing means different things at different ages and stages. For the four-year-old violin student, practicing may take all of ten minutes per day. It might consist of holding the bow straight or playing a rhythm correctly for several bars. Regardless of how extensive it is, the child hears the word "practice" and a routine begins to be established. For a ten-year-old trumpet player just starting out, practicing means, among other things, buzzing through the mouthpiece for five minutes a day. For students studying traditional methods, it means learning to read music at the same time he or she is learning the rudiments of the instrument.

Make sure your child clearly understands the teacher's expectations from week to week. The teacher should spell out specifically what the child needs to work on, how long they should work on it, and how many times something should be repeated (though that should take a backseat to how well they work on it). For many children, the more specific a teacher is—how many repetitions, how many measures of a piece—

the better. This will take the onus off you. A good teacher is also sensitive to the individual child's personality, learning style, attention span, and other demands (homework, sports, and personal issues) to determine how much of a practicing load a student can handle. One week's assignment for the piano student might mean learning eight bars of a new piece and sight-reading for five minutes; another week it might be polishing up the first page of a sonata.

The working trio—you, teacher, and child—should make sure the elements to be practiced are challenging yet still enjoyable enough for the child to engage in, and that they are demanding without being oppressive. Write down assignments in a special music notebook. Develop a practicing menu: alternate difficult passages with easy pieces and technical exercises, and always include music that your child really enjoys playing. Listen to your child, too—if an assignment is excessively frustrating, or the load too daunting to get through, the complaints may be justified. Don't be shy about raising these concerns with the teacher.

Be sensitive to your child's other responsibilities at home and school, and the potential for him to become overscheduled. Is he also participating in a demanding sport or hobby? If so, help your child determine priorities; children can't be expected to excel at everything or to endure relentless claims on their time. Between rehearsals, soccer practice, homework, and additional commitments, there may come a point when your family has to make a decision to let something go. But if your child clearly enjoys music and his other activities, see what you and the teacher can do to keep music practice assignments within a time frame that your child can accept.

Some teachers work on technique through the repertoire; a given piece might require a new fingering position or learning to play in a new key. Other teachers routinely give technical exercises to work on, from the earliest stages of study. Expectations and routines change as students get older and make progress.

Your child's motivators change, too, as she grows older and reaches a more sophisticated stage of musical development. Stickers and M&M's will give way to a sense of pride in personal and musical accomplishment.

Encouraging Your Child to Practice

Practicing is far too exacting an activity for most young children to bear the burden of themselves. As music teacher and author Cynthia Richards says, "The contact once a week with the teacher is usually not sufficient to sustain a young child's interest in practicing through the week or to ensure that practicing is not done incorrectly." Telling a young child to "just go practice" doesn't really work. That may have been the prevalent parental attitude a generation or two ago, but it also resulted in a lot of talented students quitting. Children live in the moment—many of them do not understand the long-range implications of regular practicing even though they might relish their immediate accomplishments.

How, then, to proceed? First, let's try to reaffirm some basic parenting skills. For instance, the larger goals lie with us as parents. We must encourage musical and self development, set boundaries while allowing specific choices and freedom within those boundaries, and be extremely supportive. Practice time should be looked at as a way to spend some special, focused time with your child; very young music students relish this togetherness. So make practicing feel like fun, not a dreaded chore. You want your child to achieve a distinct feeling of progress, yet have a spirit of playfulness about his practice. For example, we discovered that our dog has sensitive ears; he will sometimes cover his ears with both paws when my son is playing out of tune. As a result of this discovery, correcting intonation has at times taken on some ridiculous dimensions.

Watch your own attitude to keep things even-tempered, nonpunitive, and firm yet friendly. This may mean setting up a reward system (see page 146 in this chapter for suggestions), but don't be afraid to use consequences for any out-of-hand behavior, either. The main thing is to maintain the routine and expect that some practice sessions will be more productive than others, just as some will be more enjoyable.

Establishing a Practice Routine from Toddlers to Teens

It is impossible to overestimate the value of establishing a routine for children of whatever age. Here are some hints, some of which are obviously geared for younger students.

♪ Schedule practice at the same time, in the same place every day, if possible. If not, create a daily schedule that accommodates other activities but still includes practice time *before* your child is likely to be too tired.

♪ Make the practice space a special place, free of unnecessary distractions and out of the way of household traffic.

♪ Reiterate the week's daily and weekly practicing assignments.

♪ Set up a colorful chart or practice calendar that includes what the student is to practice; use stickers or stars for jobs well done.

♪ Praise small things—"Good bow hold!" or "Wow, you played that entire section without stopping!"

♪ Inject some game playing to achieve small goals ("Now show your stuffed animals how you can play that piece a second time.").

♪ Include fun pieces to work on for "dessert." This may mean a jazz tune, a Beatles song, whatever will help motivate your child.

♪ Avoid threats or punitive attitudes.

♪ Give small rewards that can be traded up once a month or so for larger rewards; for instance, twenty stickers earn a small toy.

A practice routine is just as important for older beginners, but the challenge of establishing one for preteens and teenagers is much more complex. What worked for your eight-year-old (a weekly ice cream cone or a trinket once in a while) will not cut it anymore, and predictable material rewards may not be motivating enough. On the other hand, older beginners may have chosen to study an instrument on their own or through an opportunity at school. Perhaps they are now physically ready to work on the more advanced instrument that first interested them in the past, but weren't physically ready for. Even though these students may be enthusiastic about their choice, they still need a routine. They may also need help figuring out their practice parameters.

Parental Involvement in Practicing

There are many small things a parent—whether musically trained or not—can help with that make all the difference for a child's musical progress. Felice Swados, who teaches harp and piano in western Massachusetts, has much to say about this issue.

There are parents that I have to talk to over and over and over again. They tell me how busy they are and that they have no time. Well, I understand that—but it's a matter of spending ten or fifteen minutes a day with your child—to encourage him and sit with him during practice. I had one little girl who'd been taking piano lessons for three years with various teachers, and she still hardly knew how to read music. She'd stayed at the same level—she could only read three notes, C, D, and E. So I started working on sight-reading with her. I got her a book and we sat and sight-read at every lesson. I told her to work on this every day. I called her dad, who plays the piano, several times, and said, "This is what you should do with her every day, even if it's only for a few minutes—sit down and do this with your daughter."

I did this for two years. And this kid never learned to read music, because nobody at home ever paid any attention! But when I talked to her father about it and suggested that maybe she shouldn't be taking lessons, he'd say, "But this is so important!" So it's hard to know sometimes exactly *what* parents have in their minds. This father thought that music was really meaningful, it had been meaningful in his life, and he wanted it to be meaningful to his children, but at the same time he wasn't willing to put the time in.

There are many other factors at work when it comes to practicing. Musically adept students who make rapid progress are often eager to tackle their most compelling musical problems and challenging pieces instead of avoiding them or asking to do that part after dinner or tomorrow. It is fun for them. Their drive and motivation can help guide the rest of us.

But take heart! Many prominent musicians say they resented practicing as children because they felt they could do everything already. And there are also kids who really like to practice—even if they don't practice every day or can't cover all the things they are supposed to be working on.

Tamara, a French horn player, really likes the experience of getting lost in her own sound.

When I was younger, I just started out on the mouthpiece because it took a while to find the right horn for me. I used to practice all the time and that really helped keep my lips in shape and get sounds. I don't practice every day, but when I do, I go over everything my teacher tells me to do, all the little warm-ups and everything we're working on for orchestra. I especially love playing scales. I love the way one note goes to another note. There are so many tones in between that it's kind of cool because of the way the sound changes.

Tamara's enjoyment of getting lost in her own sound is a clue that we often may not know what our children like about playing their instruments. It is also a reminder that children who like to practice scales are not abnormal—nor are children who end up really enjoying practicing. When this happens, it means you've done a good job establishing a routine and a place for music that matches their level of ability. This in turn allows them to value and derive pleasure from playing.

Personal Differences

Some music students, such as Tamara, find that practicing technical exercises is fun, providing a way to challenge themselves or show off ("How fast can I play this?"). Other music students dislike technical exercises, finding them tedious and boring. This can become the torturous side of practicing. Each child is different, and you may have to adopt utterly different strategies with different children.

Consider Elizabeth and Marc, two thirteen-year-olds from different families, who both started playing violin at an early age (four and five, respectively). Elizabeth is passionate about her violin, has been in a demanding conservatory prep program for several years, and practices several hours a day with no prompting from anyone. Marc started Suzuki training at five, and in the last few years, he has become an accomplished fiddler who has won several junior competitions in the Northeast. They each perform occasionally in professional settings—Elizabeth as a guest with regional symphonies, Mark at fiddle festivals and local venues. At this point, it's too soon to know if they will devote themselves to musical careers, though they are both advanced students. But nothing could be more different than their attitudes about practicing.

Elizabeth routinely practices two to three hours a day—and, according to her mother, she is very unhappy when she *doesn't* practice. Neither of her parents studied music or came from musical families, so it has been an education for all of them. This past year, however, homework at her school has become more demanding and time consuming. For the first time, she realized that practicing her violin when her mind is fresh is her priority.

> I now have the kind of repertoire that I need to practice two or three hours a day. But I can't push it more than that because I won't be able to do all my homework. If I do homework past 9 P.M., I'm really tired the next day. I have a lot more willpower right when I get home, so I do my practicing first. Also, to be honest, homework is easier to do when I'm tired than practice.

Yet Elizabeth manages to be a straight-A student and, like most thirteen-year-olds, she relishes her social life and her friends. She resents being considered weird or geeky because of her devotion to music. She recalls being interviewed after a concert, along with two other young musicians. "Two of us said we had a normal life and the other one said he didn't, but they ended up writing about him. It's almost like people want to think we are nerds or that we don't have any life at all, just violin, violin, violin. I see my friends a lot—and I have friends! Other kids—they do stuff too, whether it's soccer practice or some other athletic thing or Hebrew school. Everybody does stuff after school—you have things like that once you are my age."

Elizabeth, in short, serves as a valuable reminder to parents that music education does not always have to be a struggle.

Marc, however, is a different story. He is an accomplished young musician, but absolutely will not practice. Both of his parents are very involved with music; they have a family band that features Marc on fiddle, his mother on guitar, and his father on bass.

His mother wanted to help him avoid her pitfalls with music lessons as a child and give him some self-discipline and focus. She deeply regrets quitting lessons when she was young and that her parents did not push her to practice.

> I quit clarinet after one year, I quit flute after two years, I quit piano after six months, I quit guitar after about two lessons. . . . I quit everything. My parents didn't stay on my case, and I wasn't self-motivated enough to practice. I was frustrated with my own lack of "stick-to-it-iveness" so I wanted—in my adult years—to give this to Marc.

Since Marc was becoming more advanced musically, despite his practicing problems, his mother switched him to a better music school and a more demanding teacher about three years ago. That's when his resistance to practicing became a full-blown issue.

> When he started with his new teacher he was playing advanced Suzuki repertoire but was very behind in technique. He had gotten away with that earlier because he had great

intonation and a very musical way of playing, great expression. People would say, "Wow, he is good!" His new teacher clamped down on him. It was a difficult transition, but his playing has improved a lot. She holds him to a really high standard.

He doesn't complain about her—I think he really likes her, and she's very supportive, too. But he's never been a good practicer; it's been a struggle for a long time. Threats and rewards and bribes—we've tried everything. We've promised him an electric pickup for his violin—which he needs for fiddle playing—if he practices. He's dragging his heels on that, too, but he never says he wants to quit. Sometimes it seems like threats work better than rewards for him. Taking away computer privileges—that works; so does being grounded on weekends.

But maybe there is something down deep in him that knows he wants to do music. We go around and around. I say, "Do you want me to make you practice?" and he says "Yeah!" But I'm beginning to say to myself, "Do *I* want to make him practice? Is it worth the discord?" It's been very, very, very difficult.

Meanwhile, Marc clearly enjoys performing—and the fuss people make over him. "A lot of what motivates him is applause," his mother continues. "He's a good performer—but I'm afraid that he's coming up short because he won't put the time in." She continues:

> On the occasions when he knows he has to practice—for a
> performance or competition—it works out, he'll practice re-
> ally well. But when it's, "If you don't practice right now you're
> grounded for the weekend!"—it's really detrimental. The
> stuff his teacher has him working on is so difficult. "You need
> more weight in your pinky," or "Your thumb needs to be this
> much more bent." It requires such concentration, such effort.

So when he goes into his practice because I've held a gun to his head, so to speak, it becomes almost counterproductive.

What I do know is that I took lessons as a kid and my parents never made me practice, and I quit. You hear that and hear that and hear that. But I've never once heard a really accomplished musician whose parents made him practice say, "I really wish my mother hadn't made me practice so much, and I resent the fact that I can play so well."

What can we learn about practicing by looking at Elizabeth and Marc's very different cases? Plenty.

Elizabeth's experience may be exceptional. But it is her passion for playing the violin *in particular* that has propelled her and enabled her to make practicing so much a part of her life. As her mother says, she would be very unhappy if the violin were not in her life. Elizabeth's case teaches us that an important key is to encourage the passion a child has for the instrument.

Marc's musical gifts may not be as specifically tied to mastering his instrument or to playing classical music. But earlier on, his ease with the instrument and his expressive ability were intrinsically rewarding. Unfortunately he has resisted routine, and now that he is entering his teenage years, the drive to improve his skills must come from him. His mother is tired of being the musical disciplinarian, so it may be necessary for her to change strategies to encourage his improvement.

If country fiddle is where his musical passion really lies, he will figure out what he has to do to improve—but he may have to be pointed in the direction of a different kind of practicing. For example, old-time fiddlers didn't practice the way a classical musician practices, but still put in countless hours on their instruments, playing with other musicians.

The bigger lesson that Marc's story illustrates is that your own approach to your child's music lessons may have to evolve as your child matures, especially in the preteen and teenage years. What was quality time for your six-year-old may be excruciating for your ten-year-old. Parental involvement during practice sessions may have to be eliminated when your child reaches the double digits. If your routines are well-established, your children may want you nearby listening, but no longer hovering around the music stand. There will be bad days, sloppy practices, and unexpected concerns that make practice go by the wayside. Try to provide encouragement and opportunity and act as a role model by practicing your own skills—be they professional, artistic, or athletic.

Rewards, Bribery, and Honest Praise

Rewards or bribes, in whatever form, can be extremely effective. But it's important to eventually wean your child off of them.

Eve, Jonathan's mother, has found that *bribery*—and she candidly uses that term—works very well indeed.

> I know a lot of parents object to this. They say, "Oh no, we can't bribe them about everything!" But we used little things—and I ended up using things I vowed I would never do—including food! When my son was three, his teacher put a Lifesaver on the top of his bow, and he could eat it if he kept the bow straight. So it went from this at the lesson to a cookie after he practiced. And since we don't keep a lot of sweets around, he felt rewarded!
>
> Then we got a big practice chart. Every day he practiced well, he got a sticker and, at the end of thirty days, he got a small toy. Small goals and big goals—that's important, because if you only use big goals, that doesn't work, and if it's only small goals, the child stops looking forward to it. Now we are past that.

Honest praise is another simple reward parents need to remind themselves to use. Don't be afraid to correct your child during practice sessions, but remember to find something good to say. "You have to find a good balance when you help your kids practice," said Eve. "You can't criticize them for every little thing. And no matter how angry you get at your child, no matter how much fighting goes on about practicing, there has to be something good you can say even if it's just 'Good bow hold!'"

It's very important that your kids know you appreciate their efforts and their progress. The following practice tips are for children who are beyond the Lifesaver stage and can make some of their own decisions about practicing.

♪ If your child's after-school schedule varies day to day, make up a schedule that best accommodates his or her ability to concentrate. For instance, some children may not be able to practice right after playing heavy sports, but some might be able to just fine. Similarly, practicing may be more intellectually demanding than homework at times, so, depending on your child's priorities, consider scheduling practice first.

♪ Two short focused practice sessions may be more productive than one long session. Try ten minutes for technique before dinner and twenty minutes for practicing pieces after dessert.

♪ As your child progresses, let him make up his own schedule and determine what part of his practicing he can do independently.

♪ Use activities as rewards, such as playing a computer game for twenty minutes right after practice. A long-term reward (say, for a month of good practice) might mean doing something your child has been asking to do for a while, such as seeing a show, going bowling, or taking a special hike.

Suggested Reading

Canter, Lee. *Homework Without Tears*. New York: HarperResource, 1993.

Nathan, Amy. *The Young Musician's Survival Guide*. New York: Oxford University Press, 2000.

Richards, Cynthia. *How to Get Your Child to Practice . . . Without Resorting to Violence*. Orem, UT: Advance Arts & Music, 1985.

Romain, Trevor and Elizabeth Verdick. *How to Do Homework Without Throwing Up*. Minneapolis, MN: Free Spirit Publishing, 1997.

Strike Up the Band

In the early 1970s, Annabelle Prager, a New York City parent, was seeking a clarinet teacher for her ten-year-old son. A well-known children's clarinet teacher rebuffed her, saying, "Children are more apt to fall in love with their instruments, with music as well, if they can participate in an ensemble. Your son doesn't go to one of the few schools in the city that has an orchestra. There is simply no place for him to play." Prager's son attended a prestigious and well-endowed private school, not a strug-

gling, underfunded public school. She marched over to the school and asked where the orchestra was. The school director's answer was "Why don't you start one?"

She did. Prager, with no experience in such an endeavor, initially spearheaded a cooperative orchestra shared between her son's and several other private schools. Word quickly spread, and the orchestra soon expanded to include public schools and became what is now known as the InterSchool Orchestras of New York (ISO). Prager quickly learned how school instrumental programs had disappeared around the country, almost overnight, due to widespread, draconian budget cuts in education. The golden age of band and orchestra programs in both public and private schools was over. By the end of the 1970s, fewer than 17 percent of New York City public schools had instrumental programs, and many did not have any music at all. Cities elsewhere had similar figures. The barometer kept falling through the 1980s.

The ISO is now in its thirty-second season and has provided opportunities and support for the thousands of students who have been through its ranks ever since. It has won several awards as an outstanding model for early classical music education. The organization includes two beginner orchestras, one intermediate orchestra, two advanced orchestras, a chamber music program, and a percussion ensemble. Three of the ISO orchestras are conducted by alumni, who, hardly coincidentally, have pursued dual careers in performance and music education.

The ISO's multitier setup is not unique among youth orchestras. Organizations including the Seattle Youth Symphony, the Greater Twin Cities Youth Orchestra, and the Greater Dallas Youth Orchestra have similar programs, which offer many advantages and opportunities to students of all different skill levels. Typically, children can enter beginning orchestras as early as second grade and can progress as members of more advanced ensembles throughout middle and high school. The children and their families constitute a community—many friendships are made among children and parents alike. The beginner groups get to hear the more advanced ensembles at various concerts and events through the year; many of the kids are then motivated to work hard to get promoted to the next level, especially when they see some of their friends move up.

Mission: Possible

There are currently between four and six hundred youth orchestras in the United States, ranging, like their adult counterparts, in size, location, scope of activities, and resources. At least two hundred of these youth orchestras fall under the auspices of the American Symphony Orchestra League, the professional support organization for American symphony orchestras. Virtually all of them are nonprofit organizations. Some, like the ISO, are independent. Some are offshoots of professional orchestras such as the St. Louis Symphony, San Francisco Symphony, or Cleveland Orchestra, or have strong affiliations with them. Some are associated with schools or universities. Some are completely initiated and run by parents. In the early 1980s, there was a huge growth spurt in the formation of new orchestras. Already established organizations started forming additional orchestras and ensembles to provide outlets for an even greater number of children, to compensate for the fewer and fewer instrumental programs available in public schools, especially in urban settings.

Many of the parent-initiated groups, including the ISO, developed, by necessity, a more professional thrust over the years. They hired executive directors and, where possible, staff members to carry out general logistics in conjunction with musical directors, coaches, and music teachers. A big part of their job is fundraising and being grant savvy. However, parent volunteers and their input are still essential to the success of these operations, for everything from additional professional and financial resources to snacks, smiles, transportation, and, above all, musical support at home.

Yet whether the locale is a big city, the suburbs, or a small town, youth orchestras of all levels essentially have the same basic mission: to provide instrumental music students an opportunity to participate in an orchestra while cultivating musical ability and hands-on classical music appreciation. These groups are intended to be supplemental where instrumental programs still exist in schools, but for many students, a youth orchestra provides the only opportunity to play in this kind of ensemble. And just as there are extramusical benefits of studying an instrument, there are additional benefits, including community involvement and new social opportunities, of playing with a band or orchestra.

Joining Up

How do you find out about these orchestras? And how do you know if your child is ready?

"One of the saddest things I hear is when someone says 'I've been looking for something like this for years,'" says Anne McKinney, executive director of the ISO. "People find us mostly through word-of-mouth or if we do an outreach program in their school."

Many students have made their way to these ensembles through friends, acquaintances, and music teachers. Also, hearing about other children's personal experiences in such groups can have a strong influence on your child.

But information gathering has improved markedly for these nonprofits because of the Internet. The American Symphony Orchestra League's Web site has a list of links to its affiliated youth orchestras, and the Web site of the Metropolitan Youth Symphony of Portland, Oregon, hosts a Web directory of youth orchestras with additional links and information. (See the end of this chapter for contact information.) Virtually all youth orchestras have their own Web sites that include detailed information about how to join, audition and skill requirements, rehearsal schedules, performances, and special events.

Participation in a youth orchestra often requires an audition, but not always. This might sound like an intimidating experience, but the reality generally is just the opposite, for organizers often seek to make auditions warm and encouraging. The idea, after all, is for children to gain exposure to this process. Children are typically asked to perform in front of two or three conductors and coaches. The process is beneficial not only for your child's musical skills but also for her social skills—she learns how to be poised, self-confident, and proud of what she can do.

Specific skill and audition requirements can vary depending on the organization, but are generally not all that stiff for beginning orchestras—so neither you nor your child should allow the prospect of auditions to intimidate you. Most beginning orchestras require that students have been playing at least a year and are continuing to take lessons. At the audition, your child will be asked to sight-read brief examples of music appropriate for the level of orchestra she is auditioning for, and to play one or two prepared pieces. She might also be asked to sight-read rhythms and demonstrate some scales. She needs to be familiar with dynamics, accents, and basic musicianship. Auditioners will take into account your child's nervousness, age, and so forth; that is, they know that she will develop greater skills and self-confidence as she goes along. Auditions also exist to place returning members—to see if a child is ready to move up in her section or to a new orchestra altogether.

Beginners' orchestras generally are made up of students with a wide variety of skill levels and ages. The organizations want participation from a broad community; children are rarely turned away unless they clearly do not have the basic skills that a specific orchestra requires. Some organizations have a quasi-official grace period to make sure that new members are adjusting well and feel confident about being in an orchestra.

How much of a time commitment is involved? Typically, these ensembles have one rehearsal a week, which runs an hour for beginning orchestras and two hours for advanced ensembles, and they perform three or four concerts a year. Students are encouraged to practice their parts at home, not just at rehearsals. Does this add up to a lot more practice time? At the beginner levels, it might mean another twenty to thirty minutes a day, when the children are learning new repertoire; for the advanced levels, it probably adds another thirty minutes and more, depending on the complexity of the pieces and whether the student is a featured soloist.

Being in an orchestra should not be viewed as an added burden for your child, and it can work in tandem with her private music lessons. For one thing, music teachers are generally happy to hear that your child is involved in something new and exciting. And secondly, your child's teacher can help her with specific technical problems with the repertoire and can suggest ways to incorporate the music into her regular practice sessions.

Many kids latch on to the challenge. Tamara, a French horn player now going into her third year with the ISO, proudly announced that she was promoted to the intermediate orchestra for next fall. She is now in seventh grade, in a noteworthy middle school that has visual arts classes but no music. The ISO provides the perfect ensemble for her level of expertise. So far, she clearly enjoys it. "I love the orchestra—I love listening to the different sounds, I love just sitting there," Tamara said. "I like the challenge of not being able to tell what sound I am making, of blending in. It's like getting trapped in a maze, and it's so much fun that you don't want to leave." Her experience in the orchestra has given her the self-confidence and motivation to work hard over the next year to audition for one of the city's premier arts and music high schools.

Aside from the musical experience, the social value of youth orchestras is terrific. Music making feels cooperative and fun and encourages the kind of close-knit camaraderie found among the members of a sports team. Friendships are forged through rehearsals, performances, trips, and post-concert celebrations. The kids of different ages, backgrounds, and from different locations get to interact with each other. Some of them travel great distances to be involved, whether it's an hour-long subway ride or a car trip from one outlying neighborhood to another.

Children's orchestras can represent the payoff for studying orchestral instruments. Here, the students are among peers, who can complain and laugh together about practicing woes, get encouragement, and finally sense that what they are doing is cool. That can mean watching older boys arrive at rehearsal on their skateboards with their instrument cases strapped to their backs or trading wisecracks with the conductor. It also means legitimately staying out late on some school nights for performances, and getting to perform at inspiring cultural venues such as Carnegie Hall, the Hollywood Bowl, or the Kennedy Center in Washington, D.C.

Several youth orchestras perform at festivals in Europe or participate in cultural exchanges with youth orchestras in other countries. For students in some areas of the country, such as Dallas, where listening to classical music is not the norm—despite a historically acclaimed symphony orchestra and world-class wind symphony—that means appreciating classical music at the source.

"We expose them to wonderful opportunities," says Charles Moore, the executive director of the Greater Dallas Youth Orchestra. Moore continues,

> We tour internationally. We've hit Germany, Poland, France—areas where music is an extremely important part of the culture. We've been in settings where music is much more appreciated than it is here. And we are very closely associated with the Dallas Symphony—they provide us with mentors and coaches, they go to concerts. Their conductor does an annual guest appearance with us. We have those relationships and a similar pairing on the wind symphony level—they'll do a side-by-side concert with us.

This process gives the students a broader exposure to musical culture than they get in their schools.

The Greater Dallas Youth Orchestra was founded in 1972 by parents, educators, and members of the Dallas music community. At first there was one orchestra with thirty-five students; there are now six orchestras that offer training to almost four hundred young musicians, age five to eighteen. It also sponsors a summer chamber music camp for young string players. The organization does not have a problem recruiting students—it's more the opposite. It doesn't always have the resources to start new groups or fill in all the gaps among schools in the large metropolitan area it serves.

The Dallas organization does fill in a couple of gaps that are different from its East Coast counterparts. "We are situated in the marching band capital of the world in Texas," says Moore.

There is this enormous band network, and there are fantastic band opportunities in the suburbs, but they are not as strong in the core cities. So we have always filled a niche for those students who have no band or orchestra programs in their schools, or for those who want something more serious than the marching bands, and with more reasonable schedules— those band directors can be pretty demanding in terms of time commitment. We've also provided a niche for students who are home-schooled. This is new, and a growing trend since I've been here. Their parents look to organizations such as ours for their children's only music ensemble opportunity.

A cautionary word: though participating in a youth orchestra or some kind of ensemble is a positive motivating experience for many children, you might not always find the right situation for your child in your area. For example, if your child is not quite up to an intermediate or advanced ensemble but is obviously beyond the beginner group, it might be wise to keep practicing, work on similar repertoire, and try again next year.

Furthermore, not every ensemble leader stresses practicing the music at home as part of personal practice—rehearsals might be frustrating for the child who knows his part while everyone else is still learning theirs. One parent unhappily remarked about her son's regional orchestra, "For my son, the orchestra is boring and group is boring. They work on ensemble skills—it's not challenging for him, and the other sections don't learn their parts—so he just has to sit there while they catch up, which is excruciating for him." This family's frustration is exacerbated by the way their all-day Saturday program is administered. "A quartet or trio would be great for him," his mother continues, "with kids who are matched in skill and motivation—but then in our school you have to do it in addition to all the other stuff. I wish we could do the chamber program instead of orchestra."

It can be very frustrating for you as a parent if you find yourself in one of these either/or situations with music programs, especially if it is one you are paying for and not an in-school program. Be your child's advocate for the ensemble setting that will keep him involved, motivated, and happy about making music with other kids.

Other Opportunities

Outreach efforts, for lack of sufficient advertising resources, time, and staff, don't always reach out far enough. Yet in big cities, there are many schools that are unaware of the range of possibilities—from starting instrumental programs to supplementing what already exists. With shoestring budgets, organizations such as the ISO have to be imaginative and resourceful. They have learned to barter with each other and with local institutions, coming up with clever ideas that meet a variety of needs and providing new links to young people who want musical expertise.

These organizations can be hotbeds of creative ways to get kids started in music and keep them interested. One idea that's taken hold and fills several niches simultaneously is the Seattle Youth Symphony's Endangered Instruments program (mentioned in chapter 4). The symphony, which was founded in 1942, started this program in two middle schools in 1990. The aim was twofold: to help restart instrumental training in middle schools that no longer provided it, and to encourage children to learn instruments that are no longer commonly taught yet are essential to symphony orchestras. The instruments singled out in this program are bassoon, oboe, trombone, tuba, French horn, viola, and string bass.

The program's success has enabled kids in many middle schools in the Seattle area to get training on these instruments. Typically, the students receive free instruction and instrument loans for the first year; in return, they have to audition for placement in one of the Seattle organization's orchestras the following year. This concept has spread to other youth orchestras, as well as to several community music schools and other organizations. This is an outstanding opportunity for teens, one that says, loud and clear, "you are needed."

Still another unusual organization is the New Jersey Intergenerational Orchestra, which pairs children with adults. Founded eleven years ago, it was the brainstorm of a violinist and music educator. The group's mission was to bring together adults and children in an orchestral setting, to advance musical learning and skills, and to provide a social opportunity for all ages—a highly unusual situation in our culture, outside of family situations. The organization now has about one hundred musicians in three orchestras—beginner, intermediate, and advanced—as well as a chamber orchestra for advanced players. It welcomes all comers—the youngest member is in first grade and the eldest is eighty-plus years old. Mixing ages, generations, and levels of experience makes this orchestra a unique entity.

"We have journalists, teachers, people from all walks of life who come after work for rehearsal—but we've managed to keep the balance between adults and children without doing anything in terms of recruiting," said Susan, the current executive director. Her eleven-year-old daughter has performed with the orchestra for three years. She continues:

> My daughter loves it—we, as a family, are very musical, so she has grown up with this—it's all around her. She could be in the New Jersey Youth Symphony, but she chooses to be in this because it's less competitive, it's more about enjoying the music. But I must say our oldest members are our best practicers—they have more time! The kids are trying to balance studying an instrument with school, soccer, and all those other things. But we provide a great service—getting all these people together of different ages and from all walks of life. We all learn something, and our musicality has been improving over the years.

Music outreach programs and youth orchestras also try to capture the interest of minority students and increasingly diversified communities. The Sphinx Organization, based in Detroit, aims to broaden the reach and appeal of classical music for African American and Hispanic students. It sponsors a variety of programs, including instrumental instruction and music appreciation programs for underserved students, and develops mentoring relationships for young African American and Latino musicians on a professional track to help give them visibility at crucial stages of their careers. From the Top, the radio showcase for outstanding young classical musicians, also has a mentorship program that matches musicians who perform on the show with young students in their communities.

Edging Up

In the advanced-level youth orchestras, auditions are more competitive among the students themselves, even though the overall feeling remains one of camaraderie and team spirit. The audition process now feels like an introduction to real-life orchestra culture, in which players get seat assignments according to their strength and sound. This is an education in how orchestras really work. They experience what it takes to be first chair and lead the section, while still aiming for excellence together.

Some of the advanced tiers of youth orchestras across the country offer first-rate, even conservatory-level playing experiences. They are perceived as hard to get into—even though the organizations are as welcoming as ever. This is indeed true in the case of the New York Youth Symphony, now in its forty-first year and one of the preeminent youth orchestras in the country. Its members are from the tri-state area and range in age from twelve to twenty-two, though most are high school students. It performs three concerts a year at Carnegie Hall that pair a work by an aspiring young composer with a classic orchestral work, and has garnered several awards for adventurous programming.

"We have very motivated kids," says executive director Barry Goldberg. "It can't just be that you've been browbeating them—they have to want to do this. The kids like to be treated as professionals—and we raise the bar. The more you challenge them, the better they'll be. We get kids who make decisions here about career paths, and some of them get hooked. It's a good place to determine where you are with your music."

A similar top-tier organization is the American Youth Symphony in Los Angeles, which also runs an extensive outreach program in the city's public schools. The majority of advanced-level youth orchestras provide excellent playing experiences for students (who may not be on a conservatory or professional track at all) and are natural stepping stones from their respective junior orchestras.

The Jazz Angle

There are many kids who find their way to jazz through their classical studies and vice versa. The spirit, history, and improvisational nature of jazz has its own pull on students, especially teenagers. The jazz band tradition has made major headway in high school programs across the country, and one can witness the outstanding results of this through the Essentially Ellington High School Jazz Band Competition, now in its eleventh year. Sponsored and developed by Jazz at Lincoln Center, the event has become far more than a competition. It fosters mentoring relationships with jazz professionals and clinicians through the course of the school year, and, for the thousands of bands all over the United States that participate, it offers, in effect, an Ellington curriculum. It focuses not only on Duke Ellington the composer, but also on the way his musicians cultivated their unique sound as a jazz big band. Every year the contest gets narrowed to fifteen finalist bands; to date, more than two hundred thousand students have performed Duke Ellington's music through this program. Recent finalists were from high schools all over the country, including Washington State, Texas, Wisconsin, Ohio, and New York.

Grow Your Own

What can you do as a parent if your school has no instrumental program? Find other parents who share your interest in getting something going. See what kind of resources might be available. Many school PTAs take it upon themselves to hire part-time music teachers; some of them have managed to start recorder clubs and guitar classes during recess time or for an after school class. A few years ago, I read about a man who had been a violinist in the Hong Kong Symphony and was so dismayed that there was no music in his daughter's elementary school in Queens, New York, that he went out and bought fifty small-size violins and started a modified Suzuki program himself. Violinist Roberta Guaspari started a string program in an East Harlem elementary school, which has since become Opus 118, Harlem School of Music, providing string lessons and ensemble programs for hundreds of inner-city schoolchildren. The movie *Music of the Heart* dramatized her successful efforts.

You may also want to try forming a small chamber group in your home with the parents and kids you know, and see what music you can create together.

If you sense that there is enough interest and need among children in your community for a band or orchestra, try to tap into whatever regional or community orchestra or chamber groups already exist in your area and encourage them to help take this on. Today, arts organizations and nonprofit organizations compete with each other for funding, so it is always a good idea to try to bolster support from an existing musical organization and perhaps start an educational program—there may be untapped grant possibilities available for this kind of partnership. Contact your regional or state arts councils for information about what resources already exist, or seek out energetic people who may share your interest.

Ensembles can't be all things for all people, nor can they accommodate all levels of talent among the children. For instance, the city of Tyler, Texas, ninety miles from Dallas, has a community orchestra and is working to improve the Tyler Youth Orchestra, but it still can't match the level of its most advanced students. "We have a couple of students who drive from Tyler every week to participate in our orchestra," says Moore, director of the Greater Dallas Youth Orchestras. "I know that happens in other areas, too—we call it the dedicated commute. But there are other smaller symphony operations that have taken on the task of supporting youth orchestras. It is incredibly rewarding. People are so grateful for this, students appreciate what they are being given—people are treated appropriately. You feel like you are doing something valuable."

Resources

American Symphony Orchestra League (ASOL)
33 West 60th Street, 5th floor
New York, NY 10023
(212) 262-5161
www.symphony.org
Publications include the *Youth Orchestra Handbook* and the *Youth Orchestra Profile Survey*, guidance and information for new and would-be organizations and administrators.

American Youth Symphony Orchestra
2376 Westwood Boulevard, 2nd floor
Los Angeles, CA 90064
(310) 234-8355
www.AYSO.org

Directory of Youth Orchestras on the Web
Hosted by the Metropolitan Youth Symphony, Portland, Oregon
www.metroyouthsymphony.org
Web links to more than 100 American and international youth orchestras; related links and resources, including links to noteworthy summer music camps and programs.

Essentially Ellington
Jazz at Lincoln Center Education Department
33 West 60th Street, 11th floor
New York, NY 10023
(212) 258-9800
www.jalc.org

**Greater Boston
Youth Orchestras**
Boston University College
of Fine Arts
855 Commonwealth Avenue
Boston, MA 02215
(617) 353-3348
www.gbyso.org

**Greater Dallas
Youth Orchestras, Inc.**
3630 Harry Hines Boulevard
Dallas, TX 75219
(214) 528-7747
www.gdyo.org

**Greater Twin Cities
Youth Symphonies**
528 Hennepin Avenue,
Suite 404
Minneapolis, MN 55403-1810
(612) 870-7611
www.gtcys.org

**Interschool Orchestras
of New York (ISO)**
1556 Third Avenue, Suite 601
New York, NY 10128
(212) 410-0370
www.isorch.org

**Metropolitan
Youth Symphony**
4800 SW Macadam, Suite 105
Portland, OR 97239
(503) 239-4566
www.metroyouthsymphony.org

**New Jersey Intergenerational
Orchestra (NJIO)**
P.O. Box 432
Cranford, NJ 07016
(908) 656-0097
www.njio.org

New York Youth Symphony
850 Seventh Ave., Suite 505
New York, NY 10019
(212) 581-5933
www.nyyouthsymphony.org

Oakland Youth Orchestra
The Malonga Casquelourd
Center for Performing Arts
1428 Alice Street, Room 202M
Oakland, CA 94612
(510) 832-7710
www.oyo.org

**San Francisco Symphony
Youth Orchestra**
Davies Symphony Hall
201 Van Ness Avenue
San Francisco, CA 94102
(415) 552-8000
www.sfsymphony.org

**Seattle Youth
Symphony Orchestras**
11065 Fifth Ave. NE, Suite A
Seattle, WA 98125
(206) 362-2300
www.syso.org

Sphinx Organization
400 Renaissance Center,
Suite 2120
Detroit, MI 48243
(313) 877-9100
www.sphinxmusic.org

9

Sifting Through the Myths:
A Conclusion

Aristotle once pondered the value of music education for children. He found that we often have our priorities reversed when we think about this issue. We tend to ask why studying music is useful. Why should we consider music essential to a child's education? He said it is indeed useful for many things; it helps us with many things. But, he said, this is ultimately the wrong answer. The right answer is that studying music is good in and of itself. Music is one of those forms of education that "we must provide for our sons, not as being useful or essential but as elevated and worthy of free men." Of course, Aristotle's statement should include all children, not just boys, but his basic argument stands: music helps make children more fully developed human beings. It improves and coordinates all faculties including physical coordination and control, mental discipline, emotional sensitivity and expression, and humanistic engagement. Children who learn to develop all their faculties with the kind of total engagement that music requires tend to become better all-around human beings and, in the process, become good at many other things. But we teach them music so they develop as people, not because it's useful.

Some of us already know this intuitively, if we have a deep connection with music ourselves. We see the value of music for our children and know the profound impact that it has on their lives. We have no doubts that music education deserves a strong and even central role in the education of our children.

Yet, since our culture has such a consumer-based relationship with music and not a participatory one, we seem to need even more justification for including music in our children's education. Parents therefore have a twofold task as advocates for music education. The first is to press for restoration of high quality music education in our schools. The second is to attempt, as people who care deeply about creating and listening to live music, to reinvigorate our own musical culture.

Fortunately, there is currently a wealth of information and data from the newly expanded field of music research that gives parents, educators, arts advocates, and educational policymakers ample evidence that music should not get left behind as a subject. In general, recent findings indicate that studying and playing a musical instrument indeed involves an array of brain-stimulating experiences that can generate a child's increased achievement and proficiency in math skills, verbal skills, physical coordination, memory retention, and cognition. The results of several studies can help us reaffirm our instincts about the significant role music should play in a child's education and life.

The results of some of these studies, however, need qualification, as scientists and researchers will readily admit. The most well-known case in point is the Mozart Effect. The term was coined in reference to the findings of a 1993 study at the University of California at Irvine by Dr. Frances Rauscher, a psychologist (now at University of Wisconsin), and Dr. Gordon Shaw, Professor Emeritus in Brain Theory and Physics. The study itself was far more modest than the media frenzy and explosion of children's CDs and tapes that it spawned. Thirty-six college students who listened to ten minutes of a Mozart piano sonata scored higher on a simple spatial-temporal task administered right afterward than students who listened to relaxation instructions or nothing at all. The effect lasted approximately ten minutes. The study was replicated by other researchers, some of whom did not obtain the same results.

In reality, the Mozart Effect was a media concoction, a wild distortion of the study's method (for one thing, these were college students, not kindergartners), and its results. Suddenly, listening to Mozart and classical music in general was seen as the answer to the future of our children and the key to their ultimate success in life—a shortcut to high educational achievement and the right career track.

It was hardly the first time the exaggerated results of a scientific study caused exaggerated reactions. Even some politicians weighed in. In 1999, the governor of the state of Georgia arranged to give newborns and their parents a free compact disc of classical music to start getting smarter right away.

Yet on the bright side, for a brief, faddish period of time, the value of listening to classical music and being musically literate was thrust into the mainstream. And in the process, the Mozart Effect also threw a spotlight on the state of music education in our schools and families.

Today, the explosion of comprehensive music research may help keep the benefits of studying music visible at the forefront of education. The most active area of research is the link between music and academic achievement. These studies seek to measure differences between students who play instruments and control groups of students who do not play, as they are reflected in IQ tests, standardized elementary school tests, SATs, general grades, and overall school performance.

These are the indicators by which educators, principals, school boards, and policymakers decide whether music has a more substantial place in our schools—and whether fragile school budgets can support music in a meaningful way.

Another strong trend in music research concerns music and higher brain function. In the mid-1990s Dr. Gottfried Schlaug, currently Director of the Music and Neuroimaging Laboratory in Boston, found that there are striking structural differences in the brains of professional musicians compared to nonmusicians, which may result in enhanced communication between the two halves of the brain. Schlaug found that regions of the brain engaged in movement planning and execution and brain regions responsible for hearing are larger in musicians when compared to nonmusicians. His current research with children between ages six and fifteen seeks to expand on this finding. He and his colleagues are now exploring whether these structural differences in the brain are caused by the rigorous training of musicians or whether atypical brain structures from birth predispose them to music. These scientists are also exploring related questions with practical implications for all of us. For example, how much music exposure is enough to cause beneficial extramusical outcomes, such as improvements in math and verbal proficiency? Must a child study a musical instrument and practice daily? And what length of time is the right amount to practice? And what intervals are most effective? In other words, does the minimal musical exposure many of our children receive in school provide any of the same beneficial effects as long-term study of a musical instrument?

While the connection between music and neuroscience is a hot topic, there are other equally interesting studies and surveys that may produce less easily quantifiable results but still have value and resonance. For instance, a survey of high school band and orchestra directors found they most valued the opportunity for their students to experience the pursuit of excellence. Numerous other studies support the value of music's therapeutic role for people of all ages and conditions—for those suffering with depression, for the elderly, for Alzheimer's patients, for autistic and learning-impaired children, and for educationally at-risk children. Additionally, new research into the origins of music reveals that music has been a tool for communication and adaptation for many thousands of years, leading some scholars and scientists to feel that music is hardwired into our brains and is part of our biological heritage.

All of this research provides sound reasons to get your children involved in studying music. Yet we still need to remember music will not magically make our children more intelligent, less vulnerable to substance abuse, kinder people, or all-around super-kids. There are benefits and joys your children will get from engaging in activities such as playing soccer or chess, acting in a play, drawing and painting, and building things that they won't get from playing the piano, violin, or being in a band. And music shouldn't take precedence over other activities your child clearly loves and needs.

Furthermore, the transfer of certain skills or enhanced cognitive facilities is not an absolute. There is no 100 percent guarantee that if your child plays the piano, it will make her a math whiz without also doing the incremental work that goes along with that discipline. Nor is it a given that kids who are good in math are necessarily going to be virtuoso violinists. Researchers admit that their studies are not definitive, and there is far more to explore. Some of the studies involving children, for instance, do not address how other factors—prior musical training or exposure, parental involvement, and social, economic, and cultural backgrounds—may influence the outcome.

Yet it's worth noting that students from countries that place a high value on classical music, music education, and artistic accomplishment—such as Hungary, the Netherlands, and Japan—continue to have the highest scores on international math achievement tests (*1988 International Association for the Evaluation of Educational Achievement Test*; the 2004 test results showed the United States as still lagging). All three countries keep music as part of the core curriculum and provide musical instruction, both instrumental and vocal, from elementary and middle school through high school. This is at odds with the current educational trend in the United States to knock out the arts and teach toward standardized tests, despite the evidence that teaching music can help educationally at-risk children improve their performance in school and make school a happier place to be.

Musical training offers a lot of lessons—more than just what's on the music stand. As Dr. Rauscher wrote, "During a performance children must constantly turn their thoughts into action. Thought structures continually have to be updated and adjusted. The combination of constant vigilance and forethought coupled with ever-changing physical responses is an educational experience of unique value."

For parents, the good news stemming from music research confirms our hunches, and Aristotle's conclusion, that children who study music at all rigorously tend to be better cultivated humans. They have more resolve, more persistence, more self-discipline, and more wide-ranging interests, as well as a curiosity for all kinds of music and musical traditions. By reinvigorating sound musical values and bringing music making back to our children, we can help give them a richer present, and future.

Resources

The following list of recommendations for reading, listening, and viewing is partial: many of the titles listed are classic books and recordings; others are newly published or released works. Please be advised that there are many available recordings and reissues of classical masterworks and albums by noted classical and jazz musicians. Additionally, software titles and Web sites are frequently subject to change. Guides to CDs and DVDs, such as the *NPR Guide to Building a Classical CD Collection* or the *NPR Curious Listener's Guide* series, can be helpful. The national organizations included here are well established and generally keep their links and resource listings up to date.

Selected Books for Children

Barber, David W. *Bach, Beethoven, and the Boys: Music History as it Ought to Be Taught.* 10th Anniversary ed. Toronto, Ontario, Canada: Sound and Vision, 1996.

Curtis, Christopher Paul. Reprint ed. *Bud, Not Buddy.* New York: Yearling, 2002.

Friedman, Carol. *Nicky the Jazz Cat.* New York: Powerhouse Books, 2005.

Ganeri, Anita. *The Young Person's Guide to the Orchestra*. Book and CD-ROM. Narrated by Ben Kingsley, music composed by Benjamin Britten. London: Chrysalis Children's Books, 1996.

Greves, Margaret. *The Magic Flute: The Story of Mozart's Opera*. New York: Henry Holt, 1989.

Hayes, Ann. *Meet the Orchestra*. New York: Harcourt, Brace, Jovanovich, 1991.

Hughes, Langston. *Jazz*. Updated and expanded by Sanford Brown. New York: Franklin Watts, 1982.

Kalman, Bobbie. *Musical Instruments from A to Z*. New York: Crabtree Publishing Company, 1997.

Kennedy, Rosemary. *Bach to Rock: Introduction to Famous Composers and Their Music with Related Activities*. Fourth ed. New Orleans, LA: Rosemary Corporation, 2002.

Krull, Kathleen. *Gonna Sing My Head Off*. New York: Knopf, 1992.

Krull, Kathleen. *Lives of the Musicians: Good Times, Bad Times (and What the Neighbors Thought)*. San Diego, CA: Harcourt, Brace, Jovanovich, 1993.

Kuskin, Karla. *The Philharmonic Gets Dressed*. New York: Harper & Row, 1982.

Levine, Robert. *Story of the Orchestra: Listen While You Learn About the Instruments, the Music, and the Composers Who Wrote the Music!* Book and CD-ROM. New York: Black Dog & Leventhal, 2000.

Moss, Lloyd. *Zin! Zin! Zin! A Violin*. New York: Simon & Schuster, 1995.

Rachlin, Ann. *Famous Children (Series): Bach. Handel. Haydn. Mozart*. New York: Barron's Educational Series, 1992.

Ryan, Pam Munoz. *When Marian Sang: The True Recital of Marian Anderson*. New York: Scholastic, 2002.

Siberall, Anne. *Bravo! Brava! A Night at the Opera: Behind the Scenes with Composers, Cast, and Crew*. New York: Oxford University Press, 2001.

Turner, Barrie Carson. *Carnival of the Animals, by Saint-Saens.* Book and CD-ROM. New York: Henry Holt & Company, 1999.

Weik, Mary. *The Jazz Man.* New York: Aladdin, 1993.

Willard, Nancy. *The Sorcerer's Apprentice.* New York: Scholastic, 1993.

Selected Listening

By Artist

Louis Armstrong: *The Hot Fives and Sevens*

The Beatles: *Beatles '65; Meet the Beatles; Rubber Soul*

The Chieftains: *Down the Old Plank Road; The Best of the Chieftains*

Regina Carter: *Paganini: After a Dream*

Miles Davis: *Kind of Blue*

Miles Davis with the Gil Evans Orchestra: *Porgy and Bess; Sketches of Spain*

Duke Ellington: *The Cotton Club Years; The Blanton-Webster Years; The Sacred Concerts; Three Suites (includes The Nutcracker); The Best of Duke Ellington*

Ella Fitzgerald: *The Rodgers and Hart Songbook; The Best of Ella Fitzgerald*

Wynton Marsalis: *Blood on the Fields*

Mark O'Connor (violin): *Hot Swing; Heroes*

Mark O'Connor with Yo-Yo Ma and Edgar Meyers: *Appalachian Waltz*

Django Reinhardt and Stephane Grappelli: *Quintet of the Hot Club of France; Djangology*

Art Tatum: *Piano Solos*

Fats Waller: *The Joint Is Jumpin'*

By Composer

J. S. Bach: *Unaccompanied Cello Suites; Brandenberg Concertos 1–6*

Ludwig van Beethoven: *Symphonies Nos. 3, 5, 6 and 7*

Hector Berlioz: *Symphonie Fantastique*

Leonard Bernstein: *Candide; On the Town; West Side Story*

Georges Bizet: *L'Arlesienne Suite; Carmen*

Frederic Chopin: *Nocturnes; Ballades; Polonnaises*

Aaron Copland: *Appalachian Spring; Billy the Kid; Lincoln Portrait; Rodeo*

Claude Debussy: *Children's Corner; La Mer*

Paul Dukas: *The Sorcerer's Apprentice*

Antonin Dvorak: *Symphony for the New World*

Manuel de Falla: *El Amor Brujo; The Three-Cornered Hat*

George Gershwin: *An American in Paris; Rhapsody in Blue; Porgy and Bess; Piano Preludes*

Louis Gottschalk: *The Banjo*

Edvard Grieg: *Peer Gynt Suite*

George Handel: *Music for the Royal Fireworks; Water Music*

Scott Joplin: "The Entertainer," "Maple Leaf Rag," *Treemonisha*

Wolfgang A. Mozart: *Flute Concertos; Concerto for Horn; Serenade in G (Eine Kleine Nachtmusik); Symphony No. 41 (Jupiter)*

Modeste Mussorsgsky: *Pictures at an Exhibition*

Serge Prokofiev: *Peter and the Wolf* and *Romeo and Juliet* ballet suites

Rachmaninoff: *Piano Concerto*

Ravel: *Bolero; Sonata for Flute and Harp; Mother Goose Suite*

Eric Satie: *Gymnopodies*

Igor Stravinsky: *Firebird; Petrushka; Rites of Spring; Symphony for Winds*

Peter Tchaikovsky: *Nutcracker; Swan Lake; Violin Concerto No. 1*

Antonio Vivaldi: *The Four Seasons*

Selected Videos and DVDs

Amadeus: A fictionalized biography of Wolfgang Amadeus Mozart

Fame: A musical about the famed High School of Music and Art in New York City

Fantasia: Disney classic with exceptional soundtrack that includes lengthy excerpts from classical masterworks conducted by Leopold Stokowski

Fiddler on the Roof

Finian's Rainbow

Leonard Bernstein's Young People's Concerts, with the New York Philharmonic (boxed set of 9 DVDs): Historic televised programs of Bernstein's concert/lecture series

The Magic Flute: Mozart's beloved opera

Marsalis on Music: An informative and entertaining series about jazz and other styles of music

Mr. Holland's Opus: Starring Richard Dreyfus, movie based on the life of an inspiring music teacher

Music of the Heart: Starring Meryl Streep, fictionalized account of Roberta Guaspari, a dedicated violinist and teacher who started a music program in Harlem

The Nutcracker: New York City Ballet, George Balanchine, choreography

Peter and the Wolf: Royal Ballet School

The Red Violin: Follows the intricate journey of a special three-hundred-year-old violin and the musicians who play it; soundtrack features Joshua Bell on violin.

West Side Story

The Wizard of Oz

Other Resources

Catalogs/Products

The Children's Group, Inc.
(Classical Kids Series)
1400 Bayly Street
Pickering, Ontario L1W3R2
Canada
(888) 668-0242
www.childrensgroup.com

Music for Little People
P.O. Box 1460
Redway, CA 95560
(707) 923-3991 and
(800) 346-4445
www.mflp.com

Rounder Records Group
(includes Alan Lomax
Collection, Library of
Congress Archive of Folk
Culture, other labels)
Camp Street
Cambridge, MA 02140
(800) 768-6337
www.rounder.com

Smithsonian Folkways
750 9th Street NW, Suite 4100
Washington, DC 20560-0953
(888) 365-5929
www.folkways.si.edu

Music Software

Hyperscore
An innovative composition
program developed by the
Media Lab at MIT. View
Hyperscore showcase at www.
amoxifen.media.mit.edu/
hyperscore.

Maestro Music Inc.
Offers two lines of tutorial
music software that are well-
organized music fundamentals
programs for various levels.
www.wrldcon.com/maestro.

Music Ace
An entertaining and comprehensive introduction to music
fundamentals for beginners of
any age. Focuses on the basics
of pitch recognition, key signa-
tures, basic ear training, and
much more. Available through
www.harmonicvision.com.

Practica Musica
A personal music theory and
ear training tutor; award-win-
ning program that is simple,
fun, and thorough, for various
levels. www.ars-nova.com.

Music Web Sites

Informative and creative music Web sites with well-presented information about composers, instruments, conductors, and more.

www.bbc.co.uk/music/parents/

www.childrensmusicworkshop.com

www.fromthetop.org
Web site for weekly radio show featuring performances and interviews by America's top young classical musicians

www.jalc.org/educ/curriculum
Jazz for Young People Online Curriculum

www.media.mit.edu/hyperins/ToySymphony
Web site for kids and parents with innovative children's composition program and interactive musical instruments developed by the Media Lab at MIT

www.musicedge.com
A great site for teens

www.nickythejazzcat.com
Excellent site about jazz for the very young

www.nyphilkids.org
The New York Philharmonic Web site for children

www.pianoeducation.org/pnokids.html

www.playmusic.org (linked to American Symphony League's www.symphony.org)

www.scottjoplin.org
Web site for the Scott Joplin International Ragtime Foundation

www.sesamestreetworkshop.org

www.sfskids.org
San Francisco Symphony's Web site for children

www.smithsonian.org
Excellent resource for information about American music history and prominent jazz pioneers

National Organizations

American Music Conference
5790 Armada Drive
Carlsbad, CA 92008
(760) 431-9124
www.amc-music.org
Advocacy organization
dedicated to supporting the
importance of music education
for young children and music
research; provides resources
for educators, parents, and
professionals

**American Music
Therapy Association, Inc.**
8455 Colesville Road,
Suite 1000
Silver Spring, MD 20910
(301) 589-3300
Promotes public awareness of
the benefits of music therapy
to improve quality of life for
children and adults with dis-
abilities or illnesses

**American Orff-Schulwerk
Association**
P.O. Box 391089
Cleveland, OH 44139
(216) 543-5366
www.aosa.org

**American String Teachers
Association (ASTA)**
1806 Robert Fulton Drive
Reston, VA 22091
(703) 476-1316
www.astaweb.com
Sponsors several programs,
including The String Project,
a program/curriculum for
establishing string lessons
and ensembles in underserved
elementary schools

**American Symphony
Orchestra League (ASOL)**
33 West 60th Street, 5th Floor
New York, NY 10023
(212) 262-5161
www.symphony.org
Support organization for
American symphony orches-
tras and American youth
orchestras; strong advocacy
organization for music education; sponsors conferences,
educational, and arts policy
initiatives

Dalcroze Society of America
Web site with links to regional
and local offices, research,
programs for students, and
teacher training
www.dalcrozeusa.org

Directory of Youth Orchestras on the Web
Hosted by the Metropolitan Youth Symphony, Portland, Oregon
www.metroyouthsymphony.org
Web links to more than 100 American and international youth orchestras; includes links to several noteworthy summer music camps and programs

From the Top
295 Huntington Avenue, Suite 201
Boston, MA 02115
(617) 437-0707
www.fromthetop.org
Nonprofit organization that encourages and features young performers; provides information, entertainment, interaction for students, their parents, and teachers; hosts a weekly radio showcase of America's top young classical musicians

International Association for Jazz Education (IAJE)
P.O. Box 724
Manhattan, KS 66505
(785) 776-8744
www.iaje.org
Initiates programs to support appreciation of jazz and its heritage and provides leadership to educators regarding curriculum, performance, and resources

International Network of Schools for the Advancement of Arts Education (NETWORK)
173 Ridge View Drive
Berkeley Springs, WV 25411
(304) 258-1799
www.artsschoolnetwork.org
Promotes excellence in arts education; supports and serves schools and instructional programs; promotes curriculum development and new schools of the arts; provides leadership in arts education through advocacy, professional development, and communication

Jazz at Lincoln Center Education Department
33 West 60th Street, 11th floor
New York, NY 10023
(212) 258-9800
www.jalc.org

Meet the Composer
75 Ninth Avenue, 3R Suite C
New York, NY 10011
(212) 645-6949
www.meetthecomposer.org
Helps support the works of contemporary composers with a range of commissioning, residency, and educational programs, including the Music Alive Program, which facilitates the pairing of composers and performing ensembles

Music-for-All Foundation
16 Mount Bethel Road,
Suite 202
Warren, NJ 07059
(908) 542-9396
www.music-for-all.org
Committed to expanding
the role of music in education, heightening the public's
appreciation of the value of
music and arts education; provides links to other advocacy
organizations

**Music Teachers
National Association**
The Carew Tower, Suite 505
441 Vine Street
Cincinnati, OH 45202
(513) 421-1420 and
(888) 512-5278
www.mtna.org

**National Association for
Music Education**
1806 Robert Fulton Drive
Reston, VA 22091
(800) 336-3768
www.menc.org
Valuable site regarding school
music programs, National
Standards for the Arts, music
advocacy, links to resources

**National Guild of Community
Schools of the Arts (NGCSA)**
P.O. Box 8018
Englewood, NJ 07631
(201) 871-3337
www.natguild.org
Offers membership to schools
based on quality of faculty,
curriculum, facilities, community outreach, and more

National Piano Foundation
13140 Coit Road, Suite 320,
LB 120
Dallas, TX 75240
(972) 233-9107
www.pianonet.com

National Public Radio
635 Massachusetts Ave., NW
Washington, D.C. 20001
(202) 513-3232
www.npr.org
Provides a distinctive range of
musical programs, including
live concert broadcasts and
specially produced programs
such as Piano Jazz and Live at
Lincoln Center; also provides
links to resources for all
genres of music

**Organization of American
Kodály Educators**
OAKE National Office
1612 – 29th Avenue South
Moorhead, MN 56560
(218) 227-6253
www.oake.org

Suzuki Association of the Americas
P.O. Box 17310
Boulder, CO 80308
(303) 444-0948
www.suzukiassociation.org

Outreach Organizations

American Youth Symphony
2376 Westwood Boulevard,
2nd floor
Los Angeles, CA 90064
(310) 234-8355
www.aysymphony.org/outreach
Organization sponsors an
outreach program serving
approximately 1,500 low-
income elementary students
in four Los Angeles school dis-
tricts. The program consists of
an in-school ensemble concert
program and an after-school
string program

Midori & Friends
352 Seventh Avenue
New York, NY 10001
(212) 767-1300
Midoriandfriends.org
Provides comprehensive music
programs, including instrument instruction, performances, and mentoring to underserved New York City public
elementary schools

**Mr. Holland's Opus
Foundation**
15125 Ventura Blvd., Suite 204
Sherman Oaks, CA 91403
(818) 784-6787
www.mhopus.org
Instruments for students
whose schools cannot provide
them; other resources

**Opus 118 Harlem
School of Music**
103 East 125th Street,
7th floor
New York, New York 10035
(212) 831-4455
www.opus118.org
School founded to expand on
the success of its nationally
recognized In-School Music
Program that offered New
York City public school students the opportunity to obtain one-on-one and ensemble
instruction after school

Sphinx Organization
400 Renaissance Center,
Suite 2120
Detroit, MI 48243
(313) 877-9100
www.sphinxmusic.org
Dedicated to building diversity in classical music through outreach programs, mentoring programs, laureate program, and the Sphinx Symphony

VH1 Save the Music Foundation
1515 Broadway, 20th floor
New York, NY 10036
(888) VH1-4-MUSIC
www.vh1.com/partners/save-the-music
Music advocacy group dedicated to helping restore music programs in America's public schools, and raising awareness about the importance of music education

Young Audiences Inc.
(national office)
115 E. 92nd Street
New York, NY 10128
(212) 831-8110
www.youngaudiences.org
Young Audiences has developed community collaborations to support excellence in the arts for children and arts education; also has regional offices

Bibliography

Calvino, Italo. *Why Read the Classics?* Translated ed. New York, Vintage Books: 1999.

Choksy, Lois. *The Kodály Context: Creating an Environment for Musical Literacy.* Englewood Cliffs, NJ: Prentice Hall, 1981.

————. *The Kodály Method 1.* 3rd ed. Englewood Cliffs, NJ: Prentice Hall, 1999.

————. *The Kodály Method 2.* 3rd ed. Englewood Cliffs, NJ: Prentice Hall, 1999.

————. *The Kodály Method: Comprehensive Music Education from Infant to Adult.* 2nd ed. Englewood Cliffs, NJ: Prentice Hall, 1988.

Choksy, Lois, Robert M. Abramson, Avon Gillespie, and David Woods. *Teaching Music in the Twentieth Century.* Englewood Cliffs, NJ: Prentice Hall, 1986.

Cutietta, Robert A. *Raising Musical Kids: A Guide for Parents.* New York: Oxford University Press, 2001.

Dale, Monica. *Songs Without Yawns: Music for Teaching Children through Dalcroze Eurhythmics (or any method!).* Ellicott City, MD: MusiKinesis, 2003.

Deliege, I. and John Sloboda (eds.). *Musical Beginnings: Origins and Development of Musical Competence.* New York: Oxford University Press, 1996.

Habermeyer, Sharlene. *Good Music, Brighter Children: Simple and Practical Ideas to Help Transform Your Child's Life Through the Power of Music*. Rocklin, CA: Prima Publishing, 1999.

Haroutounian, Joanne. *Kindling the Spark: Recognizing and Developing Musical Talent*. New York: Oxford University Press, 2002.

Horowitz, Joseph. *Classical Music in America: A History of Its Rise and Fall*. New York: W.W. Norton, 2005.

Johnson, Julian. *Who Needs Classical Music?* London, New York: Oxford University Press, 2003.

Keene, James A. *A History of Music Education in the United States*. Lebanon, NH: University Press of New England, 1982.

Keller, Wilhelm. *Orff-Schulwerk: Introduction to Music for Children (Methodology, Playing the Instruments, Suggestions for Teachers)*. New York: Schott, 1974.

Kendall, John. *The Suzuki Violin Method in American Music Education*. Princeton, NJ: Suzuki Method International, 1985.

Machover, Wilma and Marienne Uzler. *Sound Choices: Guiding Your Child's Musical Experiences*. New York: Oxford University Press, 1996.

Marsalis, Wynton. *Marsalis on Music*. New York: W.W. Norton & Co., 1995.

McDonald, D. and G. Simons. *Musical Growth and Development: Birth through Six*. New York: Schirmer Books, 1989.

McWhorter, John. *Doing Our Own Thing: The Degradation of Language and Music and Why We Should, Like, Care*. New York: Gotham Books, 2003.

Mead, Virginia Hoge. "More Than Mere Movement." *Music Educators Journal*, January 1996.

Music and Neuroimaging Laboratory at Beth Deaconess Hospital and Harvard Medical School, The. www.musicianbrain.com.

Nathan, Amy. *The Young Musician's Survival Guide*. New York: Oxford University Press, 2000.

National Standards for Music Education. Program of National Associations for Music Education. www.menc.org/information.

Perret, Peter and Janet Fox. *A Well-Tempered Mind: Using Music to Help Children Listen and Learn.* New York: Dana Press, 2004.

Richards, Cynthia. *How to Get Your Child to Practice . . . Without Resorting to Violence.* Orem, Utah: Advance Arts & Music, 1985.

Repacholi, Betty, with Sandra Pickering. "Modifying children's gender-typed musical instrument preferences: the effects of gender and age." *Sex Roles* 45 (2001):623–643.

Robison, Paula. *The Paula Robison Flute Warmups Book.* New York: European American Music Publishers, 1989.

Sloboda, John A. *The Musical Mind: The Cognitive Psychology of Music.* Oxford, UK: Oxford University Press, 1985.

———. "Interview with. . . ." *EGTA Guitar Journal,* no. 5, 1994.

Starr, William and Constance. *To Learn with Love: A Companion for Suzuki Parents.* Knoxville, TN: Kingston Ellis Press, 1983.

Suzuki, Shinichi. *Nurtured by Love: The Classic Approach to Talent Education.* 2nd ed. Miami, FL: Suzuki Method International, 1983.

Trehub, Sandra, E., David S. Hill, and Stuart B. Kamenetsky. "Parents' Sung Performances for Infants." *Canadian Journal of Experimental Psychology* 5a, no. 4 (December 1997).

U.S. Department of Education. "Arts Education in Public Elementary and Secondary Schools: 1999–2000." Compiled by the National Center for Education Statistics (NCES).

Van der Meer, Ron and Michael Berkeley. *The Music Pack.* New York: Knopf, 1994.

Wallin, N., B. Merker, and S. Brown (eds.). *The Origins of Music.* Cambridge, MA: The MIT Press, 2000.

Warner, Brigitte. *Orff-Schulwerk: Applications for the Classroom.* Englewood Cliffs, NJ: Prentice Hall, 1991.

Winner, Ellen. *Gifted Children: Myths and Realities.* New York: Basic Books, 1996.

Index